# YOU-NICORN

30 days to find your inner
unicorn and live the life
*you love.*

## DANIELLE A. VINCENT

HAPPILY EVER AFTER PRESS

## *YOU-NICORN* ACKNOWLEDGEMENTS

This book, and this life, would not be possible without the loving support, encouragement, and all-around ass-kicking awesomeness of my husband Russell. For feeding me during endless work sprints, petting my hair, making me laugh, and most importantly, for believing in me more than I even believed in myself, thank you. It's amazing that my soulmate was just around the corner from me.* I love you more than anything. More than this lamp, or this chair, or this ashtray, or this remote control. Every single day, I marvel at us, and how every year makes us better... like cheese! Mmm, cheese.

Thank you, also, to my best friend and steadfast supporter, Teresa. This whole thing was more or less your idea, so, well, here it is, ridiculous drawings and all. I'm so grateful that we have stayed such good friends over the years. Your insight and perspective has always been both profound and honest. Also, we have fun, even when we're stuck deadly sick in a hotel room. You know what I mean.

And while we're on the topic of friends, I'd also like to thank all my super-enthusiastic friends who have watched this whole transformation, who road tested the first draft, and who gave me thoughtful feedback. It was a solo project, and then it turned into a community effort. You helped me realize that I never was truly alone in this often wild and lonely process. Thanks especially to Andrea, Beth, Krista, Belinda, Suzanne, Laura, Roxanne, Kim, and Shari, who encouraged me throughout the process. Your words meant more than I think you knew at the time. You injected nitrous into my engine when I was running out of gas.

*Hat tip to Pete Yorn

Thank you to everyone who contributed to this book. Your stories are important and I am so grateful and honored that you were willing to share them with me, and allow them to be published in the book. I hope that others will find strength in your strength. I know I sure have.

Lots of authors thank their sister, agent, and/or publisher, so it is with great efficiency that I have managed to have all three in one person: Rebecca! It seems like only a few months ago that we were hashing this out on your dining room table... oh wait! It was only a few months ago! To say this literally and figuratively couldn't have happened without you is a criminal understatement. You believed in me, coached me, encouraged me, and also, like, totally published the book. I am honored to work with you, and delighted to be family. This has been rad. Let's do another!

When the question of who would design the book came up, there was no possible answer other than "Alyssa Butler." Alyssa, you are an inspiration in infinite patience, your design skill is supreme, and you're a wonderful friend on top of all that. It is an honor to have your spirit and energy in this book. I know we will work together for years to come, and I am so blessed to have you in my life on many levels.

Abby and Brandie, your independent and combined editing skills are awesome. You stayed true to my voice, and helped me to better express myself with the intention that I had for the book. Your heart and dedication and empathy comes through in your work, and I appreciate you both so much.

Mom, I wrote this entire book while you were literally walking across Europe. You are such an inspiration in your kindness, your compassion, your perseverance, and your heart. Thank you for being such a good friend.

Dad, you have never been afraid of the big, scary projects. You never hesitate to take on the world! Thank you for believing in me and knowing that I could do whatever I set my mind to. I treasure our boisterous, meandering philosophical conversations. I know you will find your philosophical influences in this book

Speaking of books... Linda! Thank you for both being my second mom, and for talking endlessly about books, business, family, jobs, etc. I value our friendship so much.

In all, this book has been the work of many talented, passionate, encouraging, brilliant, supportive people. The act of putting words in a certain order ("writing," as it were) was just the violins in a symphony of effort. I am so blessed to be with you all.

# TABLE OF CONTENTS

## Part 1 — You-nicorn!

## Part 2 — It's an inside job

# Part 3 — Other People

# Part 4 — The tool kit

Illustrations by Danielle Vincent unless otherwise noted.

## JOIN A (FREE) *YOU-NICORN* COACHING GROUP

I want you to succeed in doing all the steps of *YOU-NICORN,* and the best way to do that is to connect with a group of likeminded people. Studies show that people who have a support network and a structured lesson plan achieve better results than people struggling to do programs solo.

Your success is so important to me that I'm organizing periodic coaching groups (on Facebook) to help you get connected with other positive, amazing people like you, who are working to improve your perspective and make plans for a more awesome, fulfilled life. The coaching groups include videos to provide deeper insight and inspiration in the daily steps.

It's the perfect time to get clear on your goals and dissolve what's standing in your way... and meet some really amazing people at the same time!

The coaching group is absolutely free, and is available on a semi-annual schedule as long as there's interest.

Go to *you-nicorn.com* to find out when the next group is starting.

## GET DAILY EMAIL REMINDERS

If you don't want to join a coaching group, or none of them fit your schedule, you can still benefit from daily reminders and videos. Visit *you-nicorn.com* to subscribe.

# Introduction...

In 2010, I got a job at The Oprah Winfrey Network. At 35, I was seemingly at the pinnacle of my career. I made six figures, had my own cubicle, led meetings and contributed to higher-led meetings, wore fancy shoes, showed up to work on time, had many important lists, and was very adult.

But instead of feeling like an adult, I felt like a kid wearing an adult's outfit. Nothing fit. This life was too big for me, too awkward, too complicated. I knew I was good at my job, but everyone around me seemed to have their lives so much more "together" than I did. They had families, and retirement plans, and a home with a mortgage. Some of them even had a house they lived in, and another house they got income from, like real adults. They had good credit. I wasn't sure I really wanted all those things, but they were markers of adulthood—and I was lacking.

When I first got the job, I was living in a two-bedroom apartment in Burbank, a town so boring its city slogan should be "Burbank: It's a place!" My boyfriend and I were watching TV every night, drinking a lot every night. Basically sitting in the "flow" equivalent of a stagnant pond. I could feel the mud sucking me in.

And this was **it**. This was what I thought everyone was supposed to be so dang excited about! I had *the* job to have, in *the* town to live in. I was making more than six figures, I was saving for retirement, I was driving a sensible car, I had friends who

 helped me feel alive... I was even proficient enough at my job that they let me be (mostly) my quirky self every day. I was at a "healthy" weight, as long as I stayed on a diet at all times.

According to my high school guidance counselors, I had

achieved the pinnacle of what I, the fairly average student who took too many years to finish college, could hope to achieve. Now, I just had to *show up* for 30 - 35 more years, and everything would be ok. I could coast toward the eventual death horizon with no concerns for the future, accepting a steady paycheck and observing the slow accumulation of my retirement so that I could eventually go home and never leave.

I figured I had better get settled with settling, because this was as good as it gets.

Sure, I was unhappy with some parts of my life—most notably that my boyfriend was vaguely nonspecific about marriage plans, and I didn't feel especially loved. Sure, he would tell me he loved me from time to time, but was he delighted by my awesomeness? No, not even a little. I think he even found me kind of annoying most of the time.

Also, and probably more importantly, I didn't even really like *him*. He was miserable in his work but afraid to change jobs. He wanted to travel, and had stories from the adventures of his youth, but seemed to see those days as behind him. In retrospect, all of the things that I didn't like about him, I really didn't like about *myself*.

Instead, we watched marathons of Anthony Bourdain having adventures we would never experience.

In moments of clarity, I think we both ached for these adventures. David had "grown up" and resigned himself to his life as a mid-level designer in a large company. But me? I wasn't so sure that my adventure was in the rear view mirror. It seemed like there was still so much to explore...

But he was *comfortable*. And my job was *comfortable*.
And like the nitrous at the dentist's office, I was
able to look through the daily-drinking haze to see
that truly *horrifying* things were happening: I was
getting older and my life was slipping away, yet
I had no interest in the life or path ahead of me.
But eh, it was probably fine. "For
now." Right? It was *fine*.

Yet daily life was boring. *So
goddamn boring.*

Many of my coworkers seemed
miserable, but at least
this is what they *wanted*.
They wanted a life where
they could show up to
a moderately dependable position, build their
401k, take 7 days of vacation per year (out of 21
allowable—you don't want people to think you're
*slacking*), hand out business cards that impressed
people, afford a house and a car, and have a stable
partnership with someone equally employed in a
steady job.

But here I was in the Oprah mecca of "Live your
best life," and I couldn't even see my "best life."
I was surrounded by articles about mapping my
dreams, making vision boards, trusting my inner

compass, and *none of this even remotely resembled my life.*

Until I decided **it should**.

Because over the couple of years I worked there, I decided to give this woo-woo super-spiritual crap a try. Nothing else was working, so why not? If I dove in and lost a couple years of my life trying out this crazy witchcraft, really, what had I lost? I wasn't in love with my life, so it wasn't like I'd be throwing away anything that didn't need some heavy fixing anyways.

I was working on all these Oprah-Deepak Chopra Meditation Challenges, Oprah's Lifeclass, and Oprah's Vision Boards... but I was only working *on* them, I wasn't actually *doing* them. But what if I decided to start believing in them and doing them for myself?

Once I started unraveling the sweater of my reality, I found worlds of other self-help books (or "shelf help" as Jen Sincero, one of the dozens of authors I read and love, says)... and then, I started watching TED talks, getting Zen page-a-day calendars, and generally fully immersing myself in these beliefs. Each one had a different angle, with varying degrees of scientific proofiness, and I sucked them all in with great interest and voracity.

Over the past five years, I have been in a self-directed intensive course of study, trying to simmer down the Big Answers about *why* I never felt adult, and if I even could feel like an adult at all, and even if I *wanted* to feel like an adult. Did I want adventures, or did I just *think* I wanted adventures? Was there something wrong with me for real, or was I just not cut out for office life? Does having a retirement account matter more than being happy in the moment? Is it worth sacrificing life for... and if so, *how much life*?

Thanks to Amazon's and Audible's "if you like this, you might also like this" algorithm, I hopped on a train without a final destination. It turns out, there are *unlimited* self-help books, and *unlimited* philosophical approaches to happiness.

I tried anything. I tried adjustments to those anythings. I kept doing what worked and discarded what didn't.

And now... and now what? Well, now I have things I only could have dreamed about.

I found and married my soulmate: Russell. He and I started a successful soap business (Outlaw Soaps), moved to a rustic A-frame house in California's historic Gold Country (it even snows up here!). I travel often and to places that are diverse and exciting (I'm going to London to do work I enjoy in a month, going on vacation in India in January, and taking a "writing vacation" in Kauai, Hawaii, in March). I'm healthy and a member of a fun community gym with like-minded, energetic classmates. I have three jobs—more than enough to satisfy my love of diverse experiences and challenging work, but not too many to take away all my leisure. I am friends with people who I believe are the most interesting, intelligent, supportive, creative people around.

Basically, I crafted the life I dreamed. I would not have believed that it was possible with the tools I had just six years ago, and I am immensely grateful for everything. I only wish I could have started sooner!

This is the book I wish I had read when I was at Oprah.

I might have been able to gain clarity about why I felt how I did, and might have been able to address my misfit feelings. I might have had a clearer North Star. I might have better orchestrated my life to avoid some of the pitfalls I encountered after I left my steady job... but overall, the path has been a worthwhile one, regardless of how long it took.

This book is about what worked *even when I didn't believe it would*, and the specific things that changed my life from being a cubicle-dweller to living on a five acre property with the husband of my dreams, two awesome dogs, a thriving business that makes people's lives better, and even two goats. And now I'm fulfilling my lifelong ambition to write a book and help other people.

I hope you find what you're looking for.

"I think every chapter could be its own book," my publisher noted last week. It's true that every one of these days is the absolutely most concentrated reduction sauce that I could possibly create. There's *so much more* to each step in this book. If you find that you'd like to further explore any of the steps, please contact me at danielleavincent. com and I'll be happy to send you down the rabbit hole of that specific task.

This is not an encyclopedia of everything I learned, but it's a step-by-step guide to the basic premises and principles. As I wrote the book, it grew and grew, and chapters got delegated to "ok, for the next book." So there could soon be a *YOU-NICORN II*, as well as a goal workbook, and more. There's just *so much*. We are infinitely complex and fascinating beings, both spiritually and practically. It literally never ends. And thank goodness, because it is such an adventure.

I couldn't have distilled or compiled these steps without the tireless work of hundreds of authors before me. I have included what I feel are the "must reads" of my studies in the references section at the back of the book. I owe them my deepest gratitude for the passion, sweat, and diligence they put into their work.

I hope this book opens all the doors in the world to you and sets you on your path to adventures beyond your wildest dreams.

Sincerely,

Danielle Vincent

Illustration by Melinda Farrar.

## WHAT THIS BOOK IS ABOUT

God, The Universal Force, or just plain old biology has specifically crafted you and your passions, interests, and desires **to live them out**, not just fruitlessly dream about them.

In this book, we're going to take a good look at where you are **right now**, where you've been, and where you want to go. You'll hopefully see how fricken' amazing you are, how much you have survived, and how competent you are at getting things done. You'll also look at what skills you need to develop in order to achieve these dreams.

I f life is a map, and YOU ARE HERE, we need to find the way to get you where you want to go. That way is through Tenacity Valley, and over "Don't Give a Damn" Mountain Pass. The bus is fueled with your vision for the rainbow-dancing unicorn you know you have inside you!

Happiness and success is attracted to certain people like metal filings are attracted to a magnet. These people have direction, vision, and motivation. This book is the first 30 days of stepping stones on a path to creating the life of your dreams.

You deserve all the happiness and success you desire.

## You don't have to believe it

In so many of the self-help books I read, a fundamental tenet is that you have to believe with all of your being that you will get what you desire, and if somehow you drop that belief for even a minute, it's all over. Your dreams are in the grinder. Sorry, you failed the faith class.

Maybe stuff works better if you believe in it, but I wouldn't know. I'm a skeptic. If this stuff was dependent on me buying in 100%, I wouldn't be writing this book.

All you have to do is go through the rote actions in this book. It's as predictable as physics. If you drop something, it'll fall to the ground. If you do the actions in this book—even some of them— your life will improve.

## You don't have to know what you want

When I was at Oprah, I was pretty sure I had what I should want, so it was hard for me to even envision a different life. Everything was based on where I was at the time, so I didn't have the appropriate framework to even know what I was really looking for. Heck, I still don't know what I'm looking for with crystal clarity. And that's ok.

If you've read self-help books in the past, and you don't know what you want, you might get stuck there. But I want you to know that it's totally ok if you don't know what will make you happy.

The path is made by walking.

Not tomorrow, today.

## You do have to do it

The only thing required of you is *action*.

Sometimes you're going to feel like this isn't working (like when we get to the meditation section). You might roll your eyes and say, "Ok, but it's not *working*. It's not *doing anything*." Right. I know. It doesn't seem to be doing anything.

But it is. I swear to God and all over the place, it totally is working.

And it's not going to be comfortable all the time. Sometimes you're just not going to want to do it. But you gotta do it anyways, because that's how the book works, frealz.

And if you go through the book and you don't feel like your life has changed, well, you can go back to your regular life, already-in-progress.

What's a month? Nothing. 30 days is nothing. If you live to be 85 years old, you'll be using 1/1020th of your life to complete this 30 day book.

If it changes your life for the better, unlocks your awesomeness, wakes you up, and gets you inspired, it's worth the effort, right? Can we just agree that 1/1020th of your time is worth A SUPREMELY AWESOME LIFE?

Of course it is. So let's get started.

Not tomorrow, **today**.

## How to use this book

HOORAY! You're getting ready to become the unicorn!

This book is organized as a 30 day, one-page-per-day exercise book, with four weeks of exercises and a weekly review at the end of each week. Most of the exercises will take less than 20 minutes. Some will take up to an hour. Some will take your lifetime, and that's ok too.

Go to you-nicorn.com to join a coaching group, subscribe to the 30 day countdown for a daily reminder of your exercise, get bonuses like "100 things to do besides watching TV," and other helpful tools.

I recommend writing all over this book. Take notes in the margins. Put little exclamation points next to lines that particularly stand out to you. This book is made to be your own work in progress.

The only exception is if this is a library book. If this is a library book, I will personally come and give you a stern talking-to for writing in this—or any—library book. God Bless The Library.

## LET'S GET CONNECTED!
Want to connect with other You-nicorns around the world? Tweet using the hashtag #younicorn! Post a photo from your adventures and check out what others have posted, too!

## I'D LOVE TO STAY IN TOUCH!
You can find me on Twitter 🐦 at @howdydanielle and on Facebook 🄵 at facebook.com/howdydanielle Find my mailing list, new books, and other updates at danielleavincent.com

## DAY 1:
# Get ready for your unicornification!

## Time is tickin' my friend

We've got no time to lose here on this massive and rapidly spinning planet, and as far as any of us know, we have only one life... and that life is confusingly and unpredictably brief. It's a tough truth, since most of us have a lot more to do than we've done, and we're running out of time to do it.

Just the other day when I was driving, a truck crossed the double yellow lines into my lane, and my first thought was "OMG NOT NOW! I'M STILL WORKING ON MY BOOK!" Thankfully, he swerved and I narrowly missed having a messy draft published posthumously.

*"Begin doing what you want to do now. We are not living in eternity. We have only this moment, sparkling like a star in our hand—and melting like a snowflake."*

**– SIR FRANCIS BACON**

What "but I haven't..." flashes into your mind when you are faced with your mortality? Gone to India? Eaten petit fours in Versailles? Made peace with your family? Written a screenplay? Heard the scrambling of dachshunds at a wiener dog race?

It's *important.* It's important not to let more days sneak by while you're doing something mundane just to pay the bills or fulfill some externally-designated obligation.

## There's nothing wrong with you

I want to be super duper clear: there's nothing wrong with you. You are alive, and that shows that you have survival skills. You're reading, which means you can read. You're even reading a self-help book about how to be a unicorn, which means you want to improve yourself *and* you believe in mythical creatures.

All these things are awesome. Again, there's nothing wrong with you. And if you are perfectly happy, and you have achieved all the things you want, I welcome you to set down this book (or give it to someone else) and have 30 days back.

However, if you do want to change your life, you should understand that your beliefs, choices, reactions, and behaviors have gotten you to where you are, and you can't get beyond this point without growth. Which is probably why you're holding this book: The Universe is saying "HERE! Take this and grow!! Pull what you can from it!" Because if you could really achieve what you want out of life with who you are today, you would have already achieved it.

No matter what you want, you're going to have to grow into the person who has it.

If you're holding this book because you are disappointed with how things are going, or if you're pretty sure you could unlock some amazingness in yourself but you aren't sure where to start, **start here.**

If you haven't set the book down, you've potentially accepted that you could maybe grow from this book, learn something, and hopefully use it to improve your life.

## You're going to have to grow, and growing is hard

In the process of growing, we have to look at places we *need* to grow, and that sometimes makes us feel small. We have to accept that we're not where we want to be, and even if we *know that* from looking around, it's still sometimes hard to look that fact straight in the eye. We might feel frustrated, insufficient, or even ashamed.

That's not going to feel great. In fact, it might feel awful. We cry in the shower and rue bad decisions we've made or hurtful things we have said, or hurtful things that have been said or done to us. But that ungreat feeling is part of life, and I promise you, double pinky swear, that you can get through it.

Feeling sad is part of the process, and it's ok. It might not feel comfortable, but it's temporary, and to get where you want to go, you have to do things you've never done. Through this book, I'm going to try to keep it fun. We're in this together.

As you know from the intro, for the past five years, I have been raking myself through some hot and heavy coals on my own self-improvement journey. At one point, I complained to a friend, "I'M NOT *THAT* MESSED UP! Why is this so much *work*? And will it ever end? Why am I so broken???"

And then I realized it was actually all kind of part of the awesome journey of life, and that I was just damn grateful to be alive and along for the ride. And then a year and a half later, I was out of the coals and decided to write a book so other people could hopefully get through the coals a little faster.

Because I know you have a unicorn in you, kicking at your insides, trying to get out. And someday soon, hopefully within the next 30 days, you're going to see that unicorn, and then everyone else is going to see that unicorn, and you're going to be so *fabulous*.

This is hard work, but I know you can get through it if you want to. It's worth it. **You** are worth it.

# Before we do anything else, I want you to make a commitment to be a unicorn.

What's a unicorn? A unicorn is a magical, shining, elusive creature bringing unique gifts (even if sometimes they're a little weird), and living life fully in that unicorn's most inspiring and incredible truth.

### 1: Unique Gifts

Everyone we admire, whether it's our grandma or Prince, is admirable because of their unique gifts. They bring their best selves to life in their most authentic way. For your grandma, that might be caring about people like no one ever cared for people before. For Prince, that might be, well, being Prince.

By the end of this book, we'll be on the path to discovering and making the best use of our own unique gifts.

### 2: Living Life Fully

That means really showing up for life. If you have a dream, and you're thinking, "Ok, but first I should..." or "Ugh, but everyone says that's impossible," you gotta go for it anyways. The future is short and getting shorter. You gotta show up.

### 3: Inspiring

When we start being our most fully shining unicorn, we have such a great opportunity to inspire others—to share our journey in a real way that shows others they can also be their own unicorn. And isn't that what we really want? An army of unicorns? Heck yeah it is!

### 4: Incredible

I almost started crying just typing this part, because it's so deeply personal to me. When you really show up to life in your unique, full, inspiring way, magic really happens. You don't have to believe me now (that's on Day 6: "Suspend your disbelief"). But I assure you that the journey you're undertaking right now is so damn worth it that I hope by the end of this book you'll be tattooing the word "incredible" on your arm.

### 5: Truth

This is the bedrock. This is where we are our most authentic, genuine, true person. This is the foundation of our core goodness, and we're going to access that and build on it.

**Doesn't that sound wonderful?** If you can achieve those things by the end of this book, wouldn't you agree that the time, energy, and attention that you put into these 30 days is worth it?

All those qualities are inside of you already, right now. You are already the person you need to be to achieve any goal you can dream.

# THE PERSON WAITING INSIDE YOU

In 1993, at the age of 28, Joanne felt like a failure. She was unemployed, divorced, and a single mother. Her own mother had recently died after a long battle with multiple sclerosis, and she was still suffering intense grief. Things looked dire, and she described herself as "poor as it is possible to be in modern Britain, without being homeless."[1] She struggled with clinical depression, and was considering suicide. To make matters worse, her estranged husband was trying to seek out Joanne and her children. She had to get a restraining order for their safety, and filed for divorce.

Unsure of what else to do and out of options, Joanne started a program so she could learn to be a teacher, and lived on government assistance while she worked on writing a story that she'd had in her mind for the past few years. While she tried to settle her baby down, she often made her way to local cafes and wrote while her baby slept.

At the age of 30, Joanne finally finished the book she had been working on. She submitted it to literary agents, over and over again, and persisted until it was accepted! Now came the work of submitting to publishing houses, though. Rejection after rejection came in. No one wanted the book. 12 rejections.

Finally, a prospective publisher handed the manuscript off to his daughter. Hooked, his daughter demanded the next chapter, so the publisher bought the book and gave Joanne a £1,500 advance, advising her to get another job, since books of that

 [1]www.newyorker.com/magazine/2012/10/01/mugglemarch

kind didn't tend to make a lot of money. The publisher printed a small run—just 1,000 copies—half of which went to libraries. Five months later, the book started getting attention and winning awards.

The book was titled *Harry Potter and the Philosopher's Stone*. Joanne—JK Rowling—was 32 years old. And, well, you probably know the rest of that story.

What made JK Rowling decide to work on her story after all that, when her career and life was adrift? She said that the idea for the entire *Harry Potter* series came to her in a train station several years earlier, in a flash. She just started working on the book when she could, and through diligence and effort, she created one of the most successful book series of all time.

There are dozens of examples of people whose real contributions to the world started "late" and took surprising turns when they put themselves in the driver's seat.

Ted Turner didn't start working on CNN until he was 40 years old. Before that, he had worked in the billboard business that his father had started (which he morphed into radio, and TV). He went on to create CNN, Turner Classic Movies, and is now the largest single philanthropic landowner in the US.

Henry Ford was a sawmill operator, and later an engineer for Edison, before he started the Henry Ford Motor Company. He founded the company when he was 40. Not only did Ford invent the first commonly-used automobile, he revolutionized production, paid above-average wages, and invented the "franchise" concept.

Donald and Doris Fisher were 44 and 38, respectively, when they founded The Gap clothing chain, after being unable to find a pair of jeans that fit Donald properly.

What contribution is waiting inside you? Don't you want to uncover it?

> *"The best time to plant a tree was 20 years ago. The second best time is today."*
>
> —CHINESE PROVERB

Through this book, I hope to help you get a glimpse into it, and start your adventure toward being the unicorn you are meant to be. No matter where you're starting, the important thing is to start now.

## Plan to succeed

People who make definite plans to execute projects are much more successful than people who don't make a plan. We're going to set ourselves up for success here, so I want you to think of a consistent time every day, whether it's over breakfast or right before you go to bed, when you'll spend about an hour working on your unicornification.

If this sounds like a lot of time, I'll just circle back to the logic that you're only going to be doing this for 30 days. It's not like you're going to finish a doctorate degree (unless that's in your plan... but for the purposes of this book). It's **only 30 days**.

> "It is not hard. Don't you dare tell us this is hard. Quitting heroin is hard. Beating cancer is hard. Drinking your coffee black. Is. Not. Hard." — Melissa Hartwig, *The Whole30*

This is a quote from the introduction to *The Whole30,* which is kind of where I started thinking of self-development in 30 day chunks. You can do *anything* for just 30 days, including a daily hour-long practice of improving your life. And then at the end of it, you get your dream life! What a fricken' GREAT DEAL!

## But what if it doesn't work?

Ah, and you've invested *all that time...* time you could have been spending doing something else! Like watching *Seinfeld* or *The Golden Girls.*

I'll tell you what: If you spend an hour per day on this, and it doesn't make you feel better about yourself, your purpose, and your life, you have my 100% support in doing something else. In fact, I have even included resources at the end of this book, since I think personal growth is a long journey, and this book is just one brick in your road.

But I think you'll find it worth your while.

# How to use this book

This book is designed to be read, digested, and acted upon in 30 sequential days. So starting *today*, commit to sitting down with this book for an hour(ish) every day, reading the day's reflection, and then completing the action steps.

For the action steps (and your journal, covered on Day 25), you'll need a notebook. I find a nice narrow-ruled, high quality notebook inspires me to bring my best thoughts and attention to my personal development. It  brings a kind of importance to what I'm working on, since I feel like I'm making a real investment in myself.

We've made a special *YOU-NICORN Journal* perfect for this. You can find it at you-nicorn.com

The action steps should take between 10 minutes and 40 minutes, depending on how deep you choose to go. I have found that for me personally, it works best if I read the action steps, go do something else (like washing dishes), and ruminate on the action steps *off* paper before returning to my notebook and completing them.

I recommend you keep your notebook to yourself. You're going to be sharing a wide berth of perspectives in this notebook, many of which, out of context, might not be appreciated by those around you.

No, we're not talkin' smack about people, we're just working out our feelings, and some of that workin' out involves writing down our negative feelings to take a good look at them.

So, like, maybe just keep this notebook in a safe, private space.

## It's okay to not be perfect

If you want to stop and spend a few days working on one step, that's ok. If you want to put the book down and pick it up again later, that's ok too. This isn't a strict regimen that you must do sequentially or it's all ruined. I *do* think it works best that way, but you do you. Life happens, and I want to be clear that it's ok.

Once you've completed the book one time, you might find it helpful to go back and review individual days from time to time (for example, I have heard that people especially appreciate the "Angry Person's Forgiveness Method" on Day 15).

# Ok, so are you ready to commit to being a unicorn? HECK YES YOU ARE!

..............................................................................

**ACTION STEPS:**

*1. Get a notebook that suits your needs.*

*2. Figure out a time every day when you can complete the day's reading and action step, and block that time off on your calendar.*

# YOU ARE HERE ☺
## (and that's amazing!)

## I don't know your life, but I know that no life is easy.

I also know that as long as you are here, with eyes and a brain to read and process these words, you have survived some seriously rough times, learned some hard lessons, been beaten up by life, fallen over, stood up, and taken steps—however stumbling and unsteady—forward.

And you deserve a medal for that.

And something tells me that you didn't stop there. After those first unsteady

"And once the storm is over, you won't remember how you made it through, how you managed to survive. And you may not even be sure, whether the storm is really over. But one thing is certain. When you come out of the storm, you won't be the same person who walked in. That is what this storm is all about."

— HARUKI MURAKAMI

steps, you kept stepping, kept walking (sometimes despite

what people believed you could or could not do), and you moved forward.

Almost everyone has experienced a crisis so profound that our days can be measured as "before crisis" and "after crisis," where the crisis was the beginning of its own story... not the story of the crisis itself, but the story of after-the-crisis. The story of those difficult first steps forward. The story of the rest of our lives.

The story of how we became survivors.

One of my biggest moments of falling over was when my dog of 12 years, Diva, died. I know that there are much worse things than going through the death of a beloved pet, but we're not getting into a "who has the worst story" competition. That's the example I'm going with because it was completely devastating for me.

She was my best friend through so many phases of my life, through boyfriends coming and going, through moving across the country and back, and many personal changes.

I cared for her and petted her soft head and velvet ears, every day for 12 years (dog sitting excepted). I watched her grow from a rambunctious one year old, to a 13 year old who could barely walk, who laid in her own excrement because she couldn't stand, and who I held in my arms while she died.

My grief was so *utterly complete.*

It was bottomless, and I was falling ever-deeper into the cold depression of loss.

I couldn't imagine a life without her.

I wasn't sure I even wanted a life without her.

And yet... I kept going. My life went on, and every day was one more day that moved me beyond that life and into a new one. Just the act of waking up each morning, walking forward, and mostly getting my work done was a profound victory showing that there could be life after Diva.

It didn't feel very victorious. But still, it was victory. Every morning I was still alive was proof that I could survive.

Do you know that feeling? Do you know the daily struggle of moving past what seems like the *impossible resistance* of grief, loss, sadness, pain, anxiety, and absence of direction?

If you know that feeling, but you are still here, you are a survivor.

## Recovering from trauma

Trauma is messy. My therapist once said, "There's no guide-book for grief."

You know those seven stages of grief that people talk about? I wish I could shove those seven stages of grief right up someone's butt. I have never seen that theory help a single person in grief to harness the raw brutality of real trauma. Trying to create a linear experience out of grief is an exercise in futility at best, and counterproductive and immensely harmful at worst.

The best most of us can hope for is just to make it out of the forest alive.

Often, we are so focused on the trauma that we forget to notice that we are, in fact, surviving it. And once we get out of it, we would rather just never speak of it again. Revisiting those old scars is hard because we remember the battle.

But it's important to look at those scars, and think "I survived that battle. And if I survived that battle, I can survive anything less hard than that." And for certain traumas, *anything* is less hard than that. We can get a lot of strength from the knowledge that we survived some brutally awful stuff, and that we continued to live after it.

Without really looking at the scars—at the battle, and the chaos and sadness, and at the recovery—we don't fully appreciate the fact that we're still here. We close the door behind us, and forget that we own that part of the house. We forget we're that strong.

## Beyond survival

It's true that what doesn't kill us makes us stronger... but first, it **hurts a lot**. And without feeling that hurt, looking at that hurt, and then looking *up from that hurt*, we won't be able to move into the strength that we have *earned*.

You're stronger than you were before you had to survive. You kept moving. Sometimes you were trudging, but you kept (and maybe keep on, depending on how fresh the trauma is) moving forward.

But life can be so much more than surviving. And damn it, I think you deserve so much more than just survival. I want you to look that trauma in the eye, and say, "I survived. I'm still here."

Life can be a full-on rainbow dance of celebration through what we can only assume is a finite and ever-diminishing span of our lives. We must not just walk forward, we must *dance forward*!

Whether you got this book for yourself, or someone gave it to you, this book ended up in your hands for a *reason*. You deserve to thrive. **You deserve to dance.**

And it's in your hands right now, both literally and metaphorically.

Today is all about celebrating our survival, acknowledging how strong we had to be to march forward when life went sideways and we wanted to sit down, and really looking ourselves in the eyes and saying, "I DID THIS. I AM OK. I AM A SURVIVOR. I AM HERE. I AM AWESOME."

# LOSING THE ABILITY TO DANCE
# BECAME HER REASON FOR SINGING

Doris Day's upbringing doesn't reflect the chipper blonde you know from her famous songs and movies. Her brother died while she was growing up, and her parents divorced when her dad cheated on her mom. She grew up during the 1930s, one of the hardest periods in American history.

She set her sights on becoming a dancer, and started a dance duo in Cincinnati. In 1937, though, those dancing dreams were crushed when she injured her leg badly in a car accident.

But Doris wasn't beaten. During her recovery, she sang along with the radio. Ella Fitzgerald inspired her, with her unique vocal ability. Day said she was fascinated by Fitzgerald's range and inflections, and would observe every detail of her voice.

Her mom noticed Doris was interested in singing, so she engaged a vocal teacher, Grace Raine, to help Doris develop her voice. Raine believed Day had tremendous potential, and gave her a huge discount on classes. This enabled Day to develop her voice and launched her career as a singer.

Doris Day went on to become one of America's best known and most skilled singers, and later actors. And it was that car crash—and the devastation of her dancing career—that made all the difference.

## From sickness to health, to a new life:
## Krista—California

I grew up in a very sheltered, guilt-ridden, overly
controlling, manic-depressive household. This is
not my greatest devastation in life so far, but the
framework that supported bringing the circumstances
of devastation upon myself. Emotional bargaining
and tiptoeing around within the confines of
"righteousness" (by my mother's definition) made up
my shallow understanding of interacting with other
humans. Growing up, friendships were forbidden
or hotly contested (lest the demonic spawn of
Satan "manipulate" me into seeing the truth of my
situation—which they eventually did, but that's
another story).

I eagerly escaped my situation at the ripe age of
17 for what I saw as my only potential salvation:
an early entry on scholarship to Florida State
University, the furthest in-state school from my
hometown, though I desperately wished to escape
the South entirely. I possessed absolutely zero
interpersonal skills, practical knowledge, or
emotional maturity with which to navigate young
adulthood. What I DID have was a stellar academic
and extracurricular record, a "gifted" IQ test, and
a "rearin'-to-go" attitude to consume absolutely

every experience that had been withheld from me, and then some.

That being said, I went "stereotypical-sheltered-girl-crazy" that first summer session, as well as the short time I survived into fall semester. The overwhelming amount of options, and first-time experience of "freedom," signed me up for a crash course on sex, drugs, and alcohol... with no understanding of moderation or bodily autonomy whatsoever.

Just five months free of my self-described prison, I fell sick. Very sick. I remember cutting my finger while opening a bottle of wine in my beyond-my-means apartment complex that I shared with my trust fund South Florida "frenemies," and the wound never healing. I remember taking a bong hit at a sorority/fraternity social (I was the "poor" black sheep, often made fun of) and not being able to breathe, coughing up pneumonia and mucus, unknowing and unaware. I remember bringing a bag of cocaine home with me for Thanksgiving ("to cope"), and not being able to touch the stuff, hiding it inside the battery compartment of my childhood alarm clock.

The extreme malaise and excruciating body aches eventually rendered me unable to walk to the bathroom. I visited my childhood pediatrician twice in this time in an attempt to return to wellness and to school (freedom), and both times encountered a dismissive "you have the flu, here's some steroids"... inadvertently (negligently?) expediting the infection. Eventually I found myself in the ICU, with a mysterious life-threatening illness that took the top doctors in the area weeks to diagnose.

The CDC later concluded (after shutting down the school gymnasium for an unknown amount of time due to the interest generated by my age and unique case), that an exceptionally antibiotic-resistant, unknown community strain of MRSA (methicillin-resistant Staphylococcus aureus—known commonly as "Staph"), had taken over my lungs and blood, also accumulating into football-sized abscesses in my left arm and leg. I won't go into too much detail here, but I was hospitalized, bedridden, and finally released to home-health with self-administered drugs for over a year, not counting the subsequent emergency appendectomy and gallstone attacks. I had four chest tubes, two abscess drains, a catheter, and morphine drip for who knows how long. I had two x-rays and a CT scan daily for some time. I suffered permanent nerve damage to my left arm and hand, and had to learn to walk, use the bathroom, and "human" again from scratch.

While this was happening, how did I feel? Honestly, I can't remember. I remember flashes of watching episodes of Scrubs on repeat, unwanted (high on opiates) visits from nuns and priests, and admonishing, untimely lectures from my mother. This was punctuated with the pain and discomfort of having people insert a PICC line, or emergency chest tubes on a CT table (with nearly no anesthetic), or attempting (and failing) to suck the fluid from my lungs that was too dense to fit through the (already alarmingly large diameter) needle/syringe. The novel mental state beforehand, during the morphine drip, and in the panicked aftermath is hard to recollect. It's either lost in my memory, or suppressed under locks and chains of emotional preservatives.

Coming out of this event, I felt like I had a chance to start over again, but never once during the ordeal had I considered that I could, or was ever going to, die. I felt my near-death experience was a cosmic gift and privilege, and I continued to justify reckless behavior in the name of it. I attempted to "give back" by switching my major from Dance & Psychology to Nursing, to Education, and back to Nursing, finally landing on Exercise Science at a new school, through a myriad of other circumstances which is, again, another story. Eventually I found that the resolution to my

39

drawn-out story of mastering my health (both mental and physical) laid in exercise, and found myself consuming every ounce of knowledge I could about the human body and its limits.

The point of discussing my wavering of self after this incident is that now I know that no devastating experience (and I have had many others since then), is a light bulb-worthy, "AHA!" moment where everything finally makes sense in the way that my childhood self saw adulthood being. Nor is it a defining event outside of my reaction to it. I had unconsciously shaped my life and coping mechanisms on being emotionally and physically detached, and now as an adult, I spend the majority of my time and mental energy working to unravel and undo it all. I see my body now as a vessel to, through constant improvement of myself, educate and inspire others to aspire and revel in achieving improved versions of themselves.

Ultimately, I survived. And I still am surviving. I've been married and remarried all before 30, suffered miscarriages, accepted infertility, and have had to balance excitement for life's experiences with devastation, to reach this place in time. My takeaway is that suffering (regardless of gravity) is a tool for those open to spiritual advancement, to grow in empathy and understanding of collective interest.

........................................................................

*In your journal, write about at least one time you fell over and survived. Write the story as a story of moving forward, not just the story of what happened. Falling down was only the first step in getting up and moving forward.*

This is not an easy exercise, and I know that. But it's important to get it out so you know that you are a survivor. You earned your stripes.

# Day 3:
# you are a person.
## (a person who does things)

You aren't a messy person. You aren't a drama queen. You aren't a loser. You aren't an alcoholic. You aren't a lawyer. You aren't broke. You aren't any one thing.*

You can do things, and you can repeatedly do things. But that doesn't make you those things, it just means that you repeatedly do those things.

*"You aren't a bad person. You are a person who has done bad things. But you're not a bad person."*

— RANDI HOKETT, ARTIST, FRIEND, & ACCIDENTAL SPIRITUAL ADVISOR

Let's unpack "I am a messy person."

What does that even mean? It means that you sometimes leave stuff around and you don't clean it up. Full stop.

Language is powerful stuff, so when we call ourselves "a messy person," it becomes a part of our identity. It reinforces our behaviors (specifically leaving stuff around and not cleaning it

*Ok, you are a unicorn, but a unicorn is a lot of different things.

up), which makes them harder to change without changing our self-professed identity (which is waaaaay harder).

Identity statements like these quickly become explanations, which become excuses, which become life sentences. "I know the house is a mess. I'm just a messy person."

(Lest you think that because I am using this example, I must keep my desk and home very tidy; that could not be further from the truth. My home and desk are piled with half-done projects, papers to review, etc. I'm using this example because I called myself "a messy person" for a long time.)

In the BBC TV program *Dirk Gently's, Holistic Detective Agency,** Todd Brotzman (played by Elijah Wood) repeatedly calls himself "a loser" and "an asshole" because of unforgivable things he has done, including but not limited to stealing money from his parents so he didn't have to work.

**Dirk:** To be totally candid, I'm a bit sick of your bullshit, Todd.
**Todd:** What?
**Dirk:** I just wish you'd stop saying you're an asshole. I don't think you are, so it comes off a bit cheap.
**Todd:** Have you not been listening to me?
**Dirk:** It's very easy to act like a jerk, and then say, "Welp! I'm a jerk and that's that." But it's not like being a werewolf, is it? It's just you making excuses for your excuses.

We all have stories we tell ourselves about our identity, and it is severely damaging to continuously tell ourselves stories about our "faulty behaviors" in ways that tie into our identity.

*Based on the Douglas Adams book, so no wonder it's fricken' brilliant.   43

It can lead to poor self-esteem, depression, and worst of all, continuation of those behaviors that we find bad.

...................................................................................

1. *In your notebook, divide the page into two columns. Write characterizations you have of yourself (i.e. "I'm a messy person") in the left column, leaving a few lines of space between each characterization, because—spoiler alert—we're going to be writing on the other side of the column.*

2. *Now, title that column, "Untrue."*

3. *Title the second column, "True."*

4. *Write accurate statements about what behavior each of these represent, including the word "sometimes" in those behavioral statements (i.e. "I sometimes leave stuff around and don't clean it up.")*

# My action steps...

| Untrue | True |
|---|---|
| I'm bad with money | I sometimes make mistakes when prioritizing how to spend and save money. |
| I'm so messy | I value working and relaxing more than cleaning up the house or my car. |
| I'm a mess and can't get my projects together | I sometimes take on so much that I work on many projects at one time, which makes me feel scattered and unfocused. |

## A Story from Juna—San Diego, California

For me, the "Self Talk" exercise is a dialogue between the hand-wringing, mascara-smeared, hysteric left-column (aka me) and the kindly aunt who lives on the other side of the page.

The left-column wails, "I'm such an anti-social loser! I'm home on a Friday night reading and eating saltine crackers with peanut butter and the worst part is I LIKE IT! That's so weird!"

And the kindly aunt shuffles over from the right-column and pats the left-column's hand, and says, "There, there dear." And she pulls a kleenex out of her cardigan pocket and hands it over and says, "Let's have some tea, and let me tell you what I see."

I see a girl (I'm a few decades past girlish, but the kindly aunt is sweet that way), a girl who tries really hard all day. A girl who puts her heart out there, and a girl who needs to power down and let her thoughts wander alone for a while. Then she'll be ready to love and live the next day.

And the kindly aunt gives another squeeze and
scoots back over to her side of the page.

And no matter what bully, or hysterical crazy
erupts on the left side, the kindly aunt can make
it better. Because she has tea and she's always
right. Because she is love.

## Self-talk is a really big deal

Would you be friends with someone who talks to you like
you talk to yourself? Who, when you lock the keys in the car,
turns to you and says, "OMG that was SO STUPID. How
could you be such a forgetful, stupid mess?" Or when you
walk past them, stops you and says, "Wow, you're so *fat*. I
can't believe you let yourself go like that. Maybe if you went
to the gym like *one* time ever, or stopped putting cake in your
mouth for three seconds, you wouldn't be such a fatass." No!
Of course you wouldn't be friends with someone who talks to
you like that (truly, I hope you wouldn't).

Yet we can be monstrously cruel to ourselves.

If we wouldn't put up with this kind of awful monologue
from someone else, why do we let it stream into our brains
unfiltered like a shit fountain?

Well, for most of us, this fecal fountain has always been in our
foyer. We're used to it. We barely even hear the poop-burbling.

Our negative self-talk is a habit, and we fall back on it easily whenever we're anxious, frustrated, or disappointed.

We recite this unfiltered, awful monologue about every perceived shortcoming, nit-picking at our self-esteem, and feeding us what we end up believing is the real truth.

In a later chapter, we'll talk about negative subconscious beliefs and how to reverse those, but for now I'll just give you a little spoiler: If you repeat something often enough, it becomes a mantra, which becomes emblazoned on your consciousness. You end up believing your own self-criticism, just through the power of repetition.

You are brainwashing yourself into hating yourself when you repeat the same negative self-talk over and over. So **don't do it**. Instead, when you catch yourself practicing negative self-talk, reframe it like you did in the action step above.

# Day 4:
# WHAT iS SUCCESS?

Before you start off on your journey to
be the most awesome version of yourself,
you gotta figure out what that means.

**P**ersonal Purpose: Is there anything more daunting to
consider? There's this idea that every person has a
personal purpose that drives them forward, creates
life fulfillment, and, when pursued, will make everything in
the world fall into place.

Pretty damn heavy, right?

I mean, that's a lot of pressure. If you don't know your
personal purpose, you're just adrift in society, not really
contributing, but not really sucking a tremendous donkey
nut either. You're just filling space until you fall into a grave
and become a worm's personal purpose.

*I BELIEVE IN YOU!*

If you're reading this book, and
are at least far enough along
to read this sentence, know
that it's ok not to have a personal
purpose (or not to know it).

My personal purpose has changed
and evolved over the years, starting

49

with "I just want to help people" and eventually getting to "I want to help people live their most interesting, fulfilling, and enriched lives, whatever that means to them, using whatever resources I have available." And that's why you're reading this book right now.

So rather than trying to lasso the moon, let's just try to define what you think "success" means.

## Defining success

Much less daunting (at least to me) is defining what success looks like. We'll go into more color about this in the goals exercises, but for now, just ponder these definitions of success and note (mentally or in your notebook) which attract you and which repel you.

For these definitions of success, remember that they're general, and that everyone's specific definitions of success are a combination of these, or none of them. Also, we all come to the table with a whole truckload of baggage, so just look at these with as much suspension of "But that's not realistic" or "But I shouldn't want that" as possible:

### 1: Money
I don't mean just "comfortable" or "secure," I mean piles of cash, to the extent that you wouldn't ever have to budget or even look at your bank account.

### 2: Power/Control
Do you want things just the way you want them without

having to compromise even a little bit? That's pretty dang powerful.

### 3: Adventure

Travel! New experiences! Strange and exciting people! The idea that no one has ever walked where your feet are walking (at least for hundreds of years). The world unfolds in a giant mystery in front of you!

### 4: Security

It's possible to have security without lots of money, and it's possible to have no security, even if you have lots of power. Security means that you know that no matter what tomorrow brings, it's going to be ok.

### 5: Fame

Well-known and admired, you are a shining beacon. People know who you are, and it matters to them what you think.

### 6: Free Time

"I just want to loaf," said my friend and colleague Ray when I asked what he wanted out of life. Ain't nothin' wrong with R&R.

### 7: Love

Last but definitely not least, having the dependable, honest, complete love of another person, and being able to return that love completely, dependably, and honestly.

Just knowing what you're attracted to—what you're motivated by—is very important. It can help you make decisions that you'd otherwise be stuck on. For example, if you're offered a pay raise without a promotion, but power and fame are important to you, a pay raise is going to feel pretty hollow.

In knowledge, there's power. I'm not saying that your definitions of success have to fundamentally drive everything you do, or that you should turn down that raise unless it's accompanied by the promotion you seek, but it's good to know what's *important* to you. For example, if you're offered a promotion without a raise, and power and fame are important to you, but money isn't, then take the damn promotion! You'll be happier with the promotion than you would if you held out for the raise.

---

**Living the dream: hitting the road as a musician: Cindy - California**

I was solidly in my dream career, traveling to music festivals, getting paid well enough, helping influence pop culture and independent musicians, and yet still getting enough vacation time to tour and/or travel with my wife. At the same time I was often working from 6am until after midnight, I was tethered to my phone at all hours, and I was stressed out all of the time about making sure that I was always on top of everything. I was cranky, impatient, not making time for myself, my family, my art, my friends. I was essentially just living to work.

I lost a number of family members in a super short time, and being with these people I loved while they were on their deathbeds literally, holding vigil with them, holding each other while we felt them pass—it made me realize that work for other people was not what I wanted to lose my time to.

Grief was the immediate reaction. And since I had two deaths happen in the week of Christmas/New Year's, I was able to take concurrent bereavement leaves. I was able to take a step back from work and just handle family business for about three weeks. Taking that space made me realize how out of whack my work/life balance was and how absolutely unhappy and not myself I had been acting/feeling for years.

After I went back to work I tried to start instilling some boundaries—only 50 hours a week. No days over 12 hours. Things like that.

But also, I started making time to write songs. I decided to finally start the solo music project I had always threatened, so now I was giving myself time to practice in addition to weekly band practice and shows. And I made an active decision, with my wife's support, that if I got laid off (since those rumors were flying anyway) that I would book a tour and use it as the jumping off point for making music my primary career.

As fate would have it, I was laid off in January of 2016. I was able to save some of my severance pay, and hit the road in July with another singer songwriter, and then again in September. By October I had an album of songs written and an active plan to travel to Victoria in January 2017 to record.

I set up an Indiegogo to fund the album production, got the record recorded, found a PR person to help me with a marketing plan, went on tour again in April, May, August, September, and October to promote the record, got some good press and am still trucking along trying to make it.

These days I've got a Patreon going which just keeps growing, I'm figuring out which gigs are worth doing in order to keep the lights on and which are worth doing to feed my soul. I'm working on the next record. And have a few pick up part-time flex jobs to fill in the gaps when I'm in town for a while.

Following your dreams is wonderful and real—but it's not easy. There is still a lot of work to do. Assume that your learning curve will be steep and hours long, but also ask for help. If you have friends doing what you've always wanted to, buy them a coffee and ask them to tell you their story. They can't do the work for you, but you can see an example of how they forged their path and sometimes that's the most important thing.

## HAPPY ACCIDENTS

Bob Ross, famous for his winter mountainscapes, had never seen a snowy mountain until he was stationed in Alaska with the military. He was from Florida, and enlisted in the Air Force when he was a young and unaware 18 years old.

Though he rose through the ranks quickly, eventually becoming a Master Sergeant, military life never quite suited Ross. He found it too aggressive for his mild personality, and swore that if he ever left, he wouldn't yell at anyone ever again.

In Alaska, to supplement his military income, Bob started bartending part-time. While he was bartending, he discovered an oil painting TV show and started studying oil painting with the host, Bill Alexander.

Ross worked on his technique of wet-on-wet painting (painting with oil paint over other oil paint that hasn't dried), and eventually found that he could make more money selling his original oil paintings than he could in the military. As soon as he could, Ross retired from his position and started painting full-time.

The sales of his paintings didn't really afford him many luxuries—like haircuts—so he got a perm to save money. That's how he ended up with his signature frizzy hairstyle.

Eventually, he got his own PBS show when he was 41, and this launched a $15 million business, which included many revenue channels (paint, books, courses, etc.). He is beloved by many and left a legacy of 403 episodes, and countless happy little trees.

Bob Ross is a perfect example of someone who followed unconventional calls of success. Though Ross was motivated by money, he was more motivated by his craft, and by spreading joy through his teaching.

*Write in your notebook about the element or elements that make up success to you, in your no-baggage and no-limits world.*

## My action steps...

I want to be wealthy enough to easily afford any things and experiences we want, without concern for budgets.

I want to be secure enough to be confident in our future and the maintenance of any lifestyle we choose.

I want to love someone and be loved. I want to be someone's best friend and life partner.

I think I want adventure, and might want fame, but I'm not sure. I haven't really explored these enough to know if I want them.

I do not care for power or free time.

# day 5:
# RHYMES WITH
## (Bad Habits)

(plaid rabbits, of course)

> "We are what we
> repeatedly do."
>
> – ARISTOTLE

I'm on Facebook. All. The. Time. It's my crutch. Especially now that I'm writing, and writing is scary, I go over to see if someone likes me or something I posted. Yes, I'm really that desperate for validation. And the more terrifying the task, the more Facebook calls to me.

Lemme tell you, writing this book is absolutely terrifying.

But perpetually seeking validation on Facebook is the *opposite* of what I need to be doing right now. That compulsive habit is actually seriously compromising my ability to realize what I believe is one of my *life callings*. That is *seriously messing up my life*.

I open this chapter with this insight into my current personal vice so you can understand that I'm coming from a place of someone who **very fully understands** what it means to be a slave to a habit. I understand the siren song of "just for a minute" or "just this once."

When people think of crippling habits, "heroin" usually would win that Family Feud round. And yes, drugs can be a habit. But whereas most of us would universally agree that heroin is a bad habit, our lives are shaped by hundreds of paper cut habits. These habits can be anything from checking Facebook when you feel anxious, to lighting up a cigarette when you get in the car. Things that maybe don't seem like such a big deal. Things we almost don't even think about when we're doing them.

These habits—these paper cuts—eventually carve out who we are and what we can accomplish. If I gave in to all of my Facebook urges, this book would *never get written*. I would have never gotten started at all.

Thankfully, I have set up a ton of systems to save me from myself.

I am writing this from outside of Pioneertown, California, which is outside of Joshua Tree. There's nothing around for *miles*, and it's about 100 degrees outside. The air is still and radiantly hot, not just outside, but even outside of this bedroom. I promised myself I wouldn't leave until I was at least *mostly* done with the book. I went grocery shopping for provisions and settled in for a long and grueling haul. I'm in the only room with air conditioning (the bedroom).

And the internet is as spotty as a pointillist painting of a dalmatian.

I keep going over to check Facebook, and keep getting to the "you have no internet connection, you addict" page. Yes, these are the lengths that I go to in order to not give in to my habit. Because I take my destructive habit *that seriously.*

## Habits are comforting

Like being petted, habits soothe us. We are designed to fall back on habits when we're doing something challenging, scary, or new. They say, "There, there. The world is scary, but here's a thing that you can do that's safe. See? Picking your nails. Don't you feel better?"

There's probably a great biological reason for this—something like being comforted inside the cave—but I don't know it. I just know that we all have autopilot mechanisms inside of us that drive us toward comforting habits when we're feeling anxious.

One of my friends smokes pot at home (don't sweat it—it's legal). She thinks it might be contributing to her depression and her weight gain, and she feels like it might also be really compromising her overall enjoyment of life. But then she's home, and the pipe is there, and the TV is on, and, well, whatever. She'll quit tomorrow. It's no big deal.

And it's true, it *is* no big deal... that one time.

But over time, her pot use has become a habit. And she doesn't really *enjoy* this habit... she's just bored, or waiting for something, or tired from the day.

We all have habits like this. Most of the time, they're no big deal. But if they're keeping you from the life you want to live, they've got to change.

## The vice squad: sex and drugs and rock 'n' roll

*Important disclaimer: This is not a health book, it's a book about living the fullest, most exciting life possible. If you are addicted to drugs and/or alcohol, please seek professional help. If you have quit drinking or doing drugs because of a health issue, please do not take this chapter as an endorsement of those behaviors. Alcohol and drugs can pose serious health threats in excess (and in some cases, in any amount), and I'm trusting you to make rational, sane, reasonable decisions about your own self care. I am not a medical professional.*

> *" [Alcohol is] the only drug in the world where, when you stop taking it, you are seen as having a problem."*
>
> – JASON VALE, *KICK THE DRINK... EASILY!*

What is the #1 thing you could stop doing today that would make it easier to reach your goals?

I think recreational use of sex, drugs, and alcohol is just FINE. I have used plenty of each, and consider myself greatly enriched because of it. So you're never going to hear a stiff prohibition message from me. Many of my icons and heroes have achieved their fame and notoriety because of the enthusiastic use of drugs and alcohol (Hunter S. Thompson, to name one). But I have come to realize that heroes and legends who enjoy drugs and alcohol to excess are by far the minority of great achievers in our time, whereas the vast majority of people who "can't get their lives together" use drugs and alcohol.

I'm not saying that you can't achieve everything you ever wanted to achieve while also thoroughly enjoying drugs and alcohol, I'm just saying it's terribly unlikely. You're going to be making it very hard on yourself, and why make things harder than they already are?

Is all drug and alcohol use bad? Eh, probably not (legality aside). Here's how to tell if you should consider quitting drugs and/or alcohol: Ask yourself, "What is one thing I could stop doing today to help me achieve my highest goals for my best life?"

For me, a year ago, the answer was "Quit habitually drinking." I had the hunch that I just wasn't doing my best work when I was hungover, so I got it in my head that I should quit drinking. This had actually been a recurring thought over the previous several years, but now that I had my own business, it was a lot more important for me to be doing my best work. Our survival depended on it.

One of my biggest concerns, which is a concern among many habitual drinkers, is that once I quit drinking, I'd never be able to drink again. I know many alcoholics who just can't drink anymore, period, at all, ever, and that was one of the

reasons I didn't want to quit (iron-
ically). If I couldn't drink ever
again, I wasn't sure I wanted
to quit.

In the course of my search
for an answer for how to
improve my life, I found
the *Whole30* diet plan,
which is an incredibly
restrictive diet (which I
recommend if you're into
that kind of thing). Part
of the *Whole30* includes
quitting drinking, which
I found to be so difficult
that I started looking for
other ways to quit, even
temporarily. I found *The 30 Day Sobriety Solution,* which
happened to coincide with the diet plan, already-in-progress.

If you have the sense somewhere in your mind that your life
would be better without drinking, I recommend the book,
*The 30 Day Sobriety Solution*. And, hey, it's 30 days too, so
you might as well pick up the book after this one is done.

I have been "sober" for more than a year (the book defines
"sober" as generally abstaining from alcohol, not complete
abstinence. I do have a glass of wine or two on special occasions, but "special occasion" no longer includes "HEY, it's
WEDNESDAY!"), and I'm happy to say that it is a vast
improvement over habitual drinking.

If you are a habitual drinker, it's worth abstaining for 30 days. If the thought of abstaining for 30 days fills you with a thought of "but how would I even do that?" you probably want to give it a try anyways, no matter what.

And if you're not habitually drinking, it *still* might be worth abstaining for 30 days. Just because, ya know, exploration is good.

## LIVING THE HORROR: STEPHEN KING'S ESCAPE FROM ALCOHOLISM

In his autobiographical book, *On Writing*, Stephen King writes about how he nearly lost his family, his career, and his life to drinking. He remembered taking out the recycling and filling up the "cans" bin that had been empty just days before. It was in that moment that he realized that he had a problem with alcohol.

As he thought back on his habit, he realized that he didn't even really remember writing *Cujo*, his famous book-turned-movie about a killer dog. One of the central characters in *The Shining* was a raging alcoholic. And yet, before that night with the recycling, he hadn't really put together the significance of his alcohol problem.

His family staged an intervention, and King had to decide whether he wanted to keep drinking and lose his family—and

## But what will I tell people if I'm not drinking? Will people find me insufferable?

First, most people won't ask, care, or notice. People are way too absorbed in their own lives to worry about whether you're having a club soda or a club soda and vodka. The fact is, it matters to YOU much more than it matters to THEM.

probably die—or whether he wanted to get serious about recovery. He chose recovery, since his family and his life were too valuable to throw in the bin along with those cans.

King has written 56 novels and is one of the most successful writers in history. He is an inspiring reminder that even the most functional, brilliant, creative people struggle mightily with addictive habits.

Second, if you DO have to give a reason, here are some perfectly acceptable answers:

- I have a lot to do tomorrow, and I started getting pretty bad hangovers even if I have one drink.
- My stomach is a little touchy today, so I'm sticking with club soda.
- It makes me so sleepy, and I'd rather feel good here hanging out with you!
- I have to drive later.
- I'm taking a break from booze right now.

If you'd like more ideas on what to say about why you're not drinking, visit danielleavincent.com/justsodaplease.

You don't have to commit to future behavior, you just have to excuse yourself out of that one night's drinking.

## Never quit quitting

I'm an ex-smoker. I used to smoke *really regularly.* I loooooved smoking.

But I knew it was bad for me, so I tried to quit over and over. I was *always* trying to quit. I knew it was an issue, but somehow I couldn't stop myself from having a cigarette every time I was around anyone who was smoking.

And then one day, it stuck. Something changed and it wasn't hard to quit smoking anymore. I just... didn't want it. I didn't want to feel that way, and (as much as was still salvageable) I didn't want to look that way. I didn't want to smell like a smoker.

> "Every now and then [I expected someone would be] suggesting to me that such extreme nicety as I exacted of myself be a kind of foppery in morals, which, if it were known, would make me ridiculous; that a perfect character might be attended with the inconvenience of being envied and hated; and that a benevolent man should allow a few faults in himself, to keep his friends in countenance."
>
> —BENJAMIN FRANKLIN

I don't know what changed (well, getting a major lung infection while traveling probably had something to do with it), but research suggests that people who repeatedly quit smoking are more likely to quit smoking forever than people who never try to quit. Did it feel like a failure when I started again? Eh, kind of. But I knew I was still going to quit. I just always kept in my mind that **quitting was important**.

So if you've tried to quit and started again, don't think of it as a failure, or like you're "just not able to quit," think of it as being one step closer to quitting for good.

## What you're covering

Much of my vice was related directly to certain mental health issues, like social anxiety and depression. If you suspect this is the case for yourself, but feel like treating your mental health issues with medication is somehow "admitting failure" or "copping out," SHUT THE HECK UP AND GET SOME MEDICAL HELP. You know what's failure? You know what's copping out? Adopting self-damaging habits so you can limp along, shortening your life by abusing these inert substances, while not *truly* enjoying your life.

If you're aware that you're self-medicating with drugs and/or alcohol, you might as well work with a professional to get yourself some prescribed medications, rather than leaning on Dr. Feelgood. Save the drugs and alcohol for recreational use only, or just stop doing them entirely.

---

## Living a richer and more fun life because of sobriety: Ellen-California

I had quit drinking off and on for several years, generally when I was beginning some type of diet or after having a few too many weekends of indulging in too much booze.

I wasn't the type of person that drank at home much unless I made a nice dinner or dined out at a fancy restaurant. What got me into trouble was social drinking either at a party or in a bar. It became really easy for that one glass to turn into four.

Each time this would happen, not only would I get tipsy or trashed, I'd end up having terrible sleep,

even if I had no more than two glasses of wine.
I would fall asleep easily and wake up alert and
ready to take on the world... just two to three
hours later (at around 2:00 in the morning) and
could not fall back to sleep.

I would lose an entire day after a night of
drinking or just having a few drinks, feeling tired
and like my brain was completely foggy.

The negative self-talk and shaming was inevitable
after a night of drinking because I was pretty
worthless, unable to hold to any commitments to
anyone else or myself.

The times I would just quit drinking for several
months in a row, my sleep would improve, I would
wake up with energy and found I was so much more
dependable.

In 2015 I was going through a lot of stress. I had
quit drinking most of the year but then permitted
myself to have drinks during a few special events
and each one I ended up drinking pretty heavily and
feeling quite terrible the next day. The last straw
was when I drank too much at a friend's birthday
party and spent the next day in bed, unable to take
care of important responsibilities. That day, I
decided I was done.

There was a lot of self-shaming and frustration. But I decided that I'd never have to shame myself again if I just made a decision not to drink. There was so much more to it than that. I had made a lifestyle change and dedicated myself to eating very healthy. I also own a skin care business that applies nutrition to skin care and I thought it would be important to practice what I preach. I was so dehydrated after drinking and it pronounced every little wrinkle on my face. So I decided it was time to fully commit to my anti-aging philosophy and be proactive about feeling awesome.

I decided to quit cold turkey and a friend told me about Hello Sunday Morning, an online community of folks who are either trying to moderate, trying to quit drinking, or have quit drinking already. I found it extremely comforting to see others who were in the same place as me—people who lost control from time to time. The support I received was extremely helpful, and at the advice of one of the members, I bought the book **Kick the Drink.. Easily** by Jason Vale. After I read the book, I had no desire to ever drink again, and never looked back. The book told me what I already knew: that alcohol is toxic, it tears apart families, causes death, destroys your liver, and quite honestly, I can think of a lot of things that taste so much better that I'd rather waste calories on.

I was done.

I spent about four months on Hello Sunday Morning
and decided to spend less time online chatting
about not drinking, and more time doing things that
I never had time to do when I was drinking. I slept
better, I lost 10 pounds, I had more energy, I had
time for all the fun projects I wanted to work on,
and going out with drinkers meant I'd have loads of
free entertainment. Plus, I was able to help people
get home safely.

Two years later, I am still happy I made the
choice. I don't miss it at all. Drinking became a
distraction from dealing with big life stuff when
I really needed to. And it helped me get through
social events that I didn't feel like attending. I
think that was the biggest one for me. Because now,
when I go to events sober that I'm not all that
jazzed about, I end up doing what's best for me:
getting home sober at a decent hour, relaxing and
enjoying good self care.

## It's also ok not to stop

I personally have found it difficult to operate at peak performance while using drugs and alcohol, but this isn't the case for everyone. I know people who are even *daily drinkers and pot smokers*, who have incorporated it into their full, rich, awesome lives. Part of what defines a great life for them is being able to drink with friends at the end of a long day, and I'm not gonna knock that. We all have our joys, and it's ok to celebrate that.

But if you have the sense that you'd get more done, be more productive, be happier, and function better in your life if you could just quit drinking, it's worth it to stop for 30 days (preferably with the aid of a book like *The 30 Day Sobriety Solution*).

..............................................................................

ACTION STEPS:

*1. In your notebook, write one thing that you could stop doing today that would help you be more productive, happier, and function better in your life.*

*2. If there's something you could start doing in its place that would be more productive, write that down too.*

day 6:
# SUSPEND
## your disbelief

This book is for skeptics because I have historically been a skeptic. I have surrounded myself with people who roll their eyes when other people (usually people in drapey clothes with lots of bracelets) say "The Universe is conspiring in your favor" and other new-agey woo-woo cliches like that.

I t's just so seriously hokey and ridiculous to believe that some unseen magic is moving things around in our favor.

Also, it's impractical. There are so many questions that I have about the whole philosophy: If The Universe is conspiring in everyone's favor, why does terrible stuff happen? How can my friend, who is a wonderful person, get cancer? Certainly THAT isn't in her favor! How can people get shot in movie theaters and nightclubs? Certainly, THAT isn't The Universe conspiring in their favor.

And even pulling back from those heavy questions, what if what I want is in conflict with what my neighbor wants? Whose favor does The Universe conspire in? Is it first-believe, first-serve? Or is the fact that my neighbor is acting greedily and selfishly going to diminish her chances of Universal Conspiracy? Or are my Universal Requests going to be demoted because I selfishly hope I get Universal Favor before her?

Am I a pawn in some Universal Conspiracy to get someone else what they want? What if I don't like that person? Or, if I want to play along, how do I get direction on how to best conspire in someone else's favor?

It's all very complicated.

There's so much I find wrong about the woo-woo philosophy, and I want to be right up front about it before we get too far into the book: **I only believe this stuff as far as it's helpful and productive. And that requires a hefty suspension of disbelief.**

The principles in this book are mostly practical, but we do sometimes wade into esoteric waters.

For the purposes of becoming a unicorn, I request that you suspend your disbelief just a leeeeetle bit. You don't need to do anything special, just give belief a chance. If I say "bad things sometimes bring good results," don't immediately jump into every circumstance where that isn't the case. Instead, try to think of situations where that *is* the case. If I say "people want to help you," don't think of every person who has ever stood in your way, or failed to help you. Instead, try to think of people who voluntarily helped you when you needed it.

I'm just saying be open and play along a little bit, because our current belief systems may not be workin' out so awesomely for us. It might be worth revisiting and refreshing those beliefs.

## It's not possible that you know everything

Are you willing to accept that there are some things that you don't understand about the world? Can you fully explain how electricity works? How magnets work? Why plants have photosynthesis and make oxygen, but animals make carbon dioxide?

I hope none of us would be naive enough to claim that we are the authority on how Everything in The World works. Even the most established, educated, and investigative scientists don't know how everything works—they only know a small sliver, and readily admit it—so how could we even begin to hope to know? If you ever want to have your mind blown by the infiniteness and unknowableness of the universe, read *Astrophysics for People in a Hurry* by Neil DeGrasse Tyson.

So how can we say with any authority that **we know for a fact** that our thoughts aren't radio waves that are picked up by a big, blobby, all-pervasive Universal Force, which coordinates things in our favor? Is it because the universe is so vast and infinite that we don't matter? Are you really sure of that? Or is it possible that the universe is capable of multitasking beyond our ability to understand?

If our minds are a web browser with too many tabs open, The Universe isn't just the computer, The Universe is *everything*.

Actually, that's a bad analogy. Because there *is no analogy*. Because we don't know, I don't know, and nobody knows.

So for the purposes of making your life better, suspend your disbelief for the duration of this book. Open your mind to any possibilities that are helpful to you (specifically those outlined in this book, for the purposes of this chapter).

1. *Close your eyes, and repeat the words,* **"I open my heart and mind to the possibilities of things beyond my belief and experience."** *Really feel into those words, and imagine your mind opening up like a window to the universe.*

2. *(Open your eyes and) look around you. Marvel at the infinite complexity of the world, of the things outside your immediate field of vision, of the things beyond that, and of everything. Sometimes this is an uncomfortable feeling, but I want you to take a moment to marvel at how mindblowingly incredible it is.*

3. *While still observing all the complexity around you, repeat,* **"I am an important and powerful part of this world. I create the reality of The Universe along with The Universe. I am made of the same stuff that created all of this."**

# WEEK IN REVIEW
## day 7:

HECK YEAH! You made it through the first week, you BADASS UNICORN, you!

Do a little dance and celebrate, because this is TRUE DEDICATION to the awesome stuff, my friend! I'm so proud of you. I'm so proud of us! I'm so proud overall! HOORAY! MUPPET ARMS!

Every week, we'll just do a little recap of what we've done so far. It's kind of your freebie, no work day. Just open up your journal and look at the stuff you've written over the past week.

## You've done some pretty impressive stuff, haven't you? HECK YEAH you have!

Part 2:
IT'S AN
INSIDE
JOB

day 8:

# GOTTA STOP SOBBING

Second to deciding to try something new at all (which led you here, so congratulations!), the most important attitude shift is the decision to take full ownership of your situation right now, and accept that everything is **as it is**.

I t doesn't matter who steered the boat onto the rocks, you have a responsibility to get yourself onto a life raft!

Don't get stuck on blaming yourself or blaming others about whose fault things are. It doesn't really matter whose fault it is, what matters is that you get to work fixing the situation right now.

No matter whether you're frustrated with your partner, or $50,000 in debt because of someone else's mismanagement of your money, or even if you're reeling from the loss of a job, the fact is that **you are where you are.**

If you're worried about finances, list all your assets and your debts, look at those columns, and say (aloud, if possible), "I am going to solve this. I am in control of this situation." And then come up with ways you can put together the money to resolve your debts, a scheduled payment plan, and the firm knowledge that you can handle it.

If you've lost your job, stop rolling around the same ol' "why" questions, and decide that you're going to use this as the opportunity to find a job that you truly enjoy. Make a list of what you want, and start looking high and low for that job.

For any difficult situation in your life right now, you have to:

**1: Identify it**

**2: Resolve to take control of it and change it**

We can step up and change things for the better, make different decisions, and feel so much more powerful about our lives.

## People really want to help you

We'll talk about this later in its own chapter, but people want to help you. Your friends, family, and even strangers will come together to support you when you show you're trying to take control of your own situations.

## When it really isn't your fault

fig. 1:
turd
sandwich

When I say that you have to take owner-ship and/or responsibility for your situation, am I saying that everything is your fault? **No, and a million times over, no.**

Life isn't fair. Really, sometime it's a turd sandwich.

My super awesome friend got cancer. Am I trying to say that's her fault? **No.**

What I *am* saying is that it's her responsibility to decide what to do with that information. Is she going to go into denial and never mention it to a soul? Start a blog to chronicle her journey so others can know what it's like to go through this? Begin manufacturing methamphetamines in an RV in the desert?

These are all options, and then beyond that, there are a million other options. And what she does with those options is the important thing.

1. In your notebook or on a blank piece of paper, write a situation that you want to change, and brainstorm every possible solution to that one problem. Really workshop the heck out of it.

2. Go through and circle three that you think are the best possible solutions, and between those three, pick the one that you want to try first.

3. Now get started on that!

# day 9:
# it's all in your mind
## (Sorry)

P robably the hardest part about all this stuff is that we're in a constant struggle with unseen forces... kind of like in *Harry Potter*... except it's inside our heads. Which is bullpoo, because that's the absolute worst place for it. Most of the time, we don't even know it's there. It's just worming its way around our head like a bunch of brain maggots.

fig. 2: brain maggots

Yeah. It's really awful.

But I found a really great way to tell if your inner brain maggots are stopping you from being your most awesome self. It's so simple, and it's 100% infallible.

Ok, so let's say you've got a clear idea of what you need to do, but you can't quite get yourself to just do it? For example, you want to save for a vacation—you've always wanted to go to Spain, and next year, you'll actually have time to go— but you find yourself clicking through your favorite shoe site even though you know you have to save that money for your trip. Do you feel compelled to buy the shoes, even though you know you really don't need them, have a pair pretty similar, and would really rather go to Spain?

Something in your mind is trying to stop you from saving money and living out your dream of travel and adventure.

In this exercise, we're going to go over all the benefits you're getting from choosing the shoes over the trip to Spain:

**1: Obviously, shoes.** The shoes are a huge benefit. Just look at those shoes! So cute!

**2: Shoes are practical.** I'll wear them every day! Spain isn't practical. Hidden belief: I don't deserve to go to Spain, because travel is for rich people.

**3: These shoes in particular are on sale, and Spain will always be there.** If I put off the trip for another year, and buy these shoes now, it won't really matter. Hidden belief: It's hard to delay gratification. I don't want to wait!

**4: Also, I'll get the shoes sooner than I'll be in Spain.** These shoes will be here in a couple days, but I won't go to Spain until next year. Hidden belief: Delaying gratification is hard. Staying home is easy.

**5: If I buy the ticket to Spain, I have to also have money to stay in places, and that's**

**overwhelming.** If I buy the shoes, I don't need to face the overwhelming amount of money needed to travel.

*Hidden belief: Budgeting is scary. If I don't have to budget for the trip, I don't have to think about how broke I am.*

### 6: Traveling itself is kind of scary, too.

*Hidden belief: Staying home is safe.*

### 7: Committing to travel with my friend means I have to count on my friend.

*Hidden belief: Counting on people is scary. Staying independent is safe.*

*A word of note to my fellow internal journeyperson: These mental blocks are often really icky and uncomfortable to work through, because they're in a hairball of guilt, shame, sadness, loss, regret, and (insert endless icky feelings here). Be gentle with yourself. You have a lifetime of being held back by these internal barriers, and it's natural to feel frustrated with yourself even as you're just looking at them.*

*We'll get to forgiving yourself in a later chapter, but for now, for Pete's sake, be gentle with yourself. You are just doing the best you can.*

See, your subconscious isn't just a jerk trying to mess up your life. It's trying to protect you from what it perceives as threats to your security and, ultimately, survival. And that's super duper helpful... for cavemen. But there's a lot about caveman life that doesn't really jive with our current culture.

Doubt that we're still driven by our caveman brains? Believe that we should have evolved beyond that by now? Ok Smartypants, think of a dog circling around and around, digging on the couch cushions, before she lays down for a nap... that's wolf behavior. My little help-less dogs exhibit wolf behavior on a regular basis, so why is it so crazy that humans are making subconscious decisions based on the same survival instincts that drove our ancestors?

I'll get to the ways to reprogram your subconscious tomor-row (it's surprisingly straightforward, because caveman brains are very basic), but the first step to fixing these brain issues is to identify them. Are there problems you're just stuck with no matter how much research, investigation, and fact-finding you put in?

If there are, you may have stubborn subconscious beliefs living in the cave of your mind, and those beliefs are secretly making a maggot brain problem back there.

## If you haven't achieved the success you're looking for, you can probably blame your beliefs

It's likely that you have spent some years in the world, and during those years, you've done some stuff. I think that's a safe assumption to make, right?

In those years, your beliefs have formed what you think is possible and what you'll go for. They have formed what you see as opportunities and what you see as setbacks. They define everything from how you dress to go to the grocery store, to whether you greet car trouble with a groan and a "how'm I gonna afford this?" or a "EEE! Maybe this is the last straw before it's time to retire ol' bessie and get myself that Audi Quattro I've been eyeing!" When you get a letter from the IRS, your beliefs define every piece of your response, from dutifully printing out the form they're missing and sending it that very day, to hiding the letter in your drawer until they send letters on different colored paper (like red, for example).

Every one of the above decisions creates outcomes, and those outcomes might not seem directly related to your beliefs when they happen ("This piece of crap car broke down and I missed the job interview. I really wanted that job!" vs. "I showed up for the interview in my snazzy car that I felt proud to pull into the parking lot," and "Well, there's another year of taxes filed without owing anything," vs. "WHAT? A LIEN?")

**Side note:** *In case you're noting that the examples above require spending money, in the case of the IRS, I can attest* *from personal experience that they're very nice, and will likely work with you to make a payment plan that you can afford. Meanwhile, shoving that paper in the drawer with all the other stuff you don't want to deal with will* **definitely** *piss them off and make things worse, including receiving the same notice on more colorful paper.*

From those outcomes, which are probably not obviously connected to your beliefs, you are where you are. You have what you have. In that way, your outer world is a direct reflection of your inner world: your beliefs.

Everything around and inside you, including some health conditions, is a result of your beliefs. For example, I have a belief that pizza and chips is more enjoyable than chicken and vegetables, and that exercise is a big ol' pain in my butt, so my knee gives me trouble when I wish it wouldn't. Because my knee gives me trouble, I elect not to go on cross-country treks. In reality, I'd probably prefer to go on treks more than I enjoy the temporary joy of pizza and chips, but these things don't seem connected when I'm faced with chips... [starts writing in my own notebook]

We looked at some light correlation earlier in the shoe example, but now the rubber is going to meet the road. We're going to check out how these limiting beliefs aren't just screwing up minor things like not going to Spain, or feeling too tired to go on a trek. We're going to look at how these limiting beliefs are screwing up *your life.*

**We are where we are because of a lifetime of beliefs.**

No matter how you feel about where you are *objectively* speaking, it only really matters how well you stack up next to your own definitions of success. If you define success as "wealthy," and you're secure in your money (but not wealthy), you're not going to feel very successful. If you define success as "lots of security," but your job is set up to give you huge payouts, followed by long, lean seasons, you're also not going to feel all that successful.

On the other hand, if your beliefs align with your definitions of success, you'll feel pretty darn spiffy about yourself in that arena. In a loving relationship, and mark success as having a life of love? Check! No limiting beliefs there!

Interestingly enough, our definitions of success are often counter-indicated by our limiting beliefs. For example, if we define success as having a life filled with love, we might believe that we are unworthy of love. *This* is a limiting belief. If our definition of success includes travel and adventure, our limiting belief might be that we are stuck in a mire of responsibility that we can't escape from. If our definition of success is financial security, we might always feel like money is scarce and uncertain (and might create scarcity and uncertainty in our lives). Our brains and beliefs sometimes are kind of weird and weaselly in this arena.

This isn't *always* the case, but it's often a good compass.

So don't be surprised if you encounter these squirrelly and weasley beliefs while evaluating your definitions of success. Tomorrow, we're going to work on reversing these weasley beliefs in a painless way that requires no intensive therapy (well, intensive therapy *optional*).

1. Since we already did the exercise of "What is Success?" in Day 4, we have a very easy and objectively-written barometer to measure our own expectations against (so handy!).

2. When you start looking at your values and definitions of success, you can start uncovering the places where you haven't quite achieved the ideal life you're looking for. Now, this isn't going to necessarily be the most fun exercise, since we're going to hear some sad trombones when we address where we want to be vs.. where we are, but I assure you, it's important and worth it.

3. Flip back in your journal to Day 4's exercise where you thought about what success was, and wrote down what was important to you. In your journal, write about how you feel you're doing in those areas. If limiting beliefs come up, be sure to reflect on those.

## Changing beliefs isn't easy

We are all survivors who have learned things. Because as humans, *we get better at survival every day.* Sometimes those survival lessons are healthy and accurate (don't get into a car with a strange man), and sometimes those survival lessons aren't healthy or accurate (men aren't to be trusted).

We are presently a stew of belief systems that have led us to exactly where we are right now. Everything from our relationship status to our financial status to our health is based on our belief systems, and these belief systems either reinforce or destroy the life we want to lead.

So if you're broke, it's because your belief systems around money aren't conducive to being wealthy. If you're single, it's because your belief systems around relationships and the gender of your preference aren't conducive to being in a relationship (intentionally or not). If you can't find or keep an enjoyable, rewarding, well-paying job, it's because your belief systems aren't compatible with finding and keeping an enjoyable, rewarding, well-paying job.

Every circumstance in our lives is the direct outcome of our belief systems, not other people, or the fates, or the economy... it all ties back into our belief systems.

In this book, we're going to use as many *helpful belief systems* as possible. Sometimes these belief systems sound inaccurate because we have entire lifetimes of belief systems already built that are based on our perspective and experiences... but these belief systems **aren't working for us**. They are creating and perpetuating a life that we don't like.

So I'm asking you to give all these **helpful beliefs** a good ol' solid belief, just on faith, just for now, just until you can give them a chance to work positively in your life.

# day 10:
# REVERSING SUBCONSCIOUS BELIEFS WITH AFFIRMATIONS

Ok, now that we've identified the sticky problems (which are really your subconscious's way of making solutions), we want to change those into positive and productive beliefs.

B ut the fact that we have these mental blocks means that just thinking "I should save for a trip to Spain" won't help us if there's a deeper voice inside telling us travel is dangerous.

This part feels outstandingly cheesy to me, but it has WORKED. I wouldn't tell you to do this if it wasn't part of the plan, so please once again suspend your disbelief and play along.

For each of these sticky problems, we're going to replace that belief with the belief we'd like to have. In order to do this, we're going to need to get all deep into our brains, waaaay back to the time when we decided those problems were legit solutions, and we're going to communicate with our subconscious in a way that it understands.

Going back to our example from yesterday, where we're trying to decide between these boots and our coveted trip to Spain, I highlighted the hidden beliefs that underlie the stated benefits:

**1: I don't deserve to go to Spain, because travel is for rich people.**

**2: It's hard to delay gratification. I don't want to wait! Staying home is easy.**

**3: Budgeting is scary. If I don't have to budget for the trip, I don't have to think about how broke I am.**

**4: Staying home is safe.**

**5: Counting on people is scary. Staying independent is safe.**

We're going to take these underlying beliefs, and write the resolution / opposite of that belief:

**1: I deserve to go to Spain. Travel and adventure is for me!**

**2: I'm happy waiting to go to Spain, because going to Spain is worth it! I'll use this time to plan my trip!**

**3:** I've got control of my finances, and I can save enough money to have the adventure I want.

**4:** Having an adventure is more important to me than being safe.

**5:** I can count on my friends.

These are the beliefs that we want to bring into our lives, and we're going to do it through repetition.

## Think of your subconscious mind like a rough piece of wood

We need to take that piece of wood, and carve it down to the shape we want, and then sand away at the beliefs with finer and finer grit sandpaper, until we get to the exact smoothness and beauty that we want.

We're going to put together some statements, and, like sanding a piece of wood, we're going to repeat those statements when our subconscious minds are closest to the surface, which is in the morning before you do anything else, and at night, before you go to sleep (since the subconscious tends to grind away at thoughts and experiences overnight).

I find that 3x5 index cards are a great way to repeat my affirmations, since I have 10 or so of them that I repeat every morning, and another 5 or so that I repeat every evening (which I'll explain below). I change out cards from time to time, when I feel like any individual concept has achieved optimal smoothness. Just for fun, I have a little card catalog of all my old affirmations, which has become hundreds of cards over the past couple years.

The subconscious doesn't understand things like the word "not," so "I'm not going to drink anymore" will just sound like "I'm going to drink anymore." Not only does that make zero sense, it almost definitely will reaffirm that you want to drink. You should write your affirmations in the positive.

So, for example, if you want to cut down on your drinking, you might have a card that says, "I love being sober and healthy. I enjoy feeling clear and vibrant! I do my best work when I'm sober, and I deserve to bring my best to my life. Life is an adventure, and I'm excited to live it to the fullest!"

The subconscious mind also really likes vivid pictures, so when you write your affirmation statements, try to write it in such a way that you can envision that outcome. If you have a photo that represents the message you're trying to convey, then it may help to include and review that. I find I have a very vivid imagination, so usually just reading my affirmations is enough to envision my desired outcome.

That said, there are various ways of writing these affirmation statements, and you should find the way that works best for you. This probably isn't going to feel *super comfortable* at first, no matter what method you use, but please just keep doing it.

Some people believe that you should write your beliefs as if the thing has already happened, for example, "I am enjoying my trip in Spain, experiencing all the wonderful sights and sounds of Spain, and taking incredible photos."

Other people claim that the brain will basically "wake up" when it reads this clearly untrue statement, and that your subconscious will recede back into the depths like the Loch Ness Monster catching the glint of a camera lens.

As a skeptic, it took me a while to warm up to the concept of stating my affirmations as if they already happened, but as a student, I have gone ahead and tried it anyways. Over time, the affirmations have become just a regular part of what happens when I am having my first cup of coffee when I wake up, and my last cup of tea when I go to bed. Because the optimal method of using them is mindless repetition (because "mindless" means that your subconscious is right there at the surface), eventually all of them blur together into a kind of morning and evening mantra.

I have found that I prefer a different kind of affirmational statement in the morning than I prefer before I go to bed, so I have two little stacks of cards. My morning cards are all about being excited, motivated, and making decisions to achieve my highest goals. These cards get me started in the right direction (even if I read them with little more than a mostly-asleep mumble). My evening cards are about having done my best today, stating that everything is right and my needs are met in that moment, and that I trust the universe is unfolding to achieve my husband's and my best interests. These cards assure me that everything is ok, and that sound sleep is not only acceptable, but appropriate. I have long had sleep problems, so going to sleep with the closing message of "I sleep soundly, knowing the universe is unfolding its highest goodness for us," helps me rest easy.

ACTION STEPS:

1. *Review your sticky beliefs, and write statements that counter those. Remember, always write your statements in the positive (avoid the word "not") and use vivid statements wherever possible.*

2. *Write the counter statements on your 3x5 cards and read them in the morning and evening. If you want to make different ones for the evening, of course do that as well.*

If you'd like help writing your affirmations, plus downloadable templates, please visit: you-nicorn.com/affirmations.

## My Action Steps...

Here are a selection of affirmations cards I made based on my sticky beliefs over the past two years:

We enjoy abundance enough to
be free from stress about
money.
We are safe, comfortable, and
happy, knowing all our needs
are easily met.
My mind and heart is at peace.

Russ and I love each other through
everything.

I am enough to keep this relationship
going. He loves me no matter what,
through good days and bad,
just the way I am.

I respect myself, and I
respect money.
I honor the time and energy
I put into money by caring
for every dollar.
Abundance is mine, and we
always have more than
enough money to get anything
we want.

I am doing great work that
makes a difference.

My attention and focus are important
and every incremental improvement
makes a difference.

Saving money is fun.
I love watching our money
grow as we build our wealth.
The tax system is a fun and
interesting puzzle for us to solve.
We are building so much wealth
it is a joy to pay taxes and
tithe. We know more will flow
our way. We are money magnets!

Everything is in my control,
and I have the strength, focus,
energy, and resources to
conquer every obstacle and setback.
I am unstoppable!

**day 11:**

# YOU JUST HAVE TO KEEP GOING

While you're working on these persistent issues, enlisting your friends to help, and generally grinding away at the burrs on your axe, there will be times when you're not delighted to be doing this work. You might feel like you're walking around with rocks in your shoes, you might wake up with headaches, you might feel irritable or morose. Random stuff might even start happening to you, like your car might get a funny noise, your clothes might not fit right, or you might find that there are foxtails in everything.

Life about this time might become kind of uncomfortable.

This is because your heart, your body, your brain, and your soul are more or less breaking in a new pair of shoes. You've been walking through this world in the comfortable, well-broken-in you for the past however-many-years. Depending on your past traumas, non-serving beliefs, and resistance to the future, you'll likely have to make some internal adjustments.

These adjustments are likely to be uncomfortable and sticky. They won't feel right, and you may have to do some self-coaching to keep yourself on track.

> *"If you're going through Hell, keep going."*
>
> –WINSTON CHURCHILL

Day 11 is a tough day, since the freshness of starting a new endeavor (this book) is starting to wear off, but you still have 19 days left to go. This is when a lot of people drop off, because *UGH,* it's *so much work.*

**But not you.** YOU are going to keep going.

## These funny things

Oh, our beliefs. OHHHHH, our beliefs.

Beliefs hang out in front of our eyes like blinders or sunglasses or 3-D glasses or those rainbow-prism glasses, and literally everything is affected by them.

A friend of mine had eye surgery about 10 years ago. You know, a pretty basic procedure at this point. But his went badly, and his cornea detached. One minute, he'd be looking at something right in front of him, and the next minute it was floating away (as his cornea floated around his eyeball—awesome.).

Our belief systems are just like this. We can lose perspective, and things that felt like they were well in our hands suddenly drift off, while other things we didn't expect start floating into our lives. Coincidences, both positive and negative, jump in from all angles like jazz-hands wielding psychopaths. *SURPRISE! JAZZ HANDS! FLAT TIRE!*

Some people claim that this is the last ditch effort of your beliefs—somehow now sentient—trying to hold on to your consciousness and stay in your life. And it might feel like that.

But I think it's much more benign, mundane, and rational.

Your perspective is changing. The things you see are changing, and the things that matter are changing. You might have gotten a flat tire before, called AAA, and forgotten about it in a few days. But now, because of *everything* (your entire perspective), your flat tire feels like an insurmountable obstacle.

Right now is the critical point: There are only two places to go from here: forward, or backward. And you don't want to go backward.

When you were a little kid, knee high to a grasshopper, a grasshopper looked *huge*. Everything looked huge! Stairs were a powerful struggle to overcome. The world was too big for your little body, and you grew because nature *compelled you to grow.* You had no choice but to ride it out and get bigger, and, with the new perspective of being bigger, grasshoppers, stairs, your childhood home, and everything else, looked smaller.

The same thing happens with your emotional perspective. The decision you make today— just continuing to read to the end of this chapter, and start the next chapter tomorrow—is absolutely *crucial* in your natural journey of growth.

Really, it *is* just as simple as keeping going.

We make a bigger deal out of it, we tell ourselves how busy we are, that we don't have time for this right now, and that really, the project that just came up and is taking all our time and attention is more important than just doing a couple more days of this book. But that's emotional resistance to growth, and today, I want you to call it out for what it is: a distraction from who you're meant to be, a distraction from your fullest life, and a distraction from [insert most exciting goal here].

Once we get over this hump of Day 11, I'm not going to say it'll be clear sailing, but you'll be a bigger person on a level that will make it all easier.

# JUST KEEP RUNNING

Phil Knight, the founder of Nike, is a runner. Not just in that he goes for faster-than-a-walks on a pretty regular basis, but he is, to his core, a runner-person. Running is a crazy sport, Knight says in his book Shoe Dog. The concept itself is both pointless, and the point of everything. It's about endurance—about running even when you don't want to keep running, usually without a clear destination, and sometimes around a flat oval track.

It's because he is a runner that he knew the secret to his business was to keep running, no matter what, even though he had no clear destination. He knew that he had to keep going, to keep his lungs expanding and collapsing, to keep his heart pumping, no matter what happened with the business. He kept moving.

Knight said that he realized early, on a jog in 1962, that this wild idea—the idea of getting shoes from Japan and reselling them in the US—would be an endurance game. He realized it was like running, and that the only thing that could cause him to fail is if he stopped. But he wasn't going to stop, because he was a runner.

During his time in business, he was pretty much perpetually broke for the first two decades, he got sued, he lost his manufacturer, he faced quality problems, and he lost both his mentor and his star athlete. His was an endurance run, and he had the endurance to make it to the finish line.

*Give yourself a pat on the back, and resolve—extra super duper resolve—to do tomorrow's exercise.*

# When things go wrong, they have gone right

W e can plan it so perfectly. We can research. We can plot. We can visualize. We can prioritize. We can strategize. But even the most perfectly plotted plans can go haywire.

> *"No battle plan survives contact with enemy."*
>
> **–HELMUTH VON MOLTKE**

M oltke was talking about war strategy, but this is really true of everything. We will never be able to control reality, and as long as we encounter reality, our plans will be out of our control. But if we have our intentions set correctly (that is, written down and focused on, which we'll talk about in the last week of this book), I believe The Universe is guiding us toward the best circumstances for our achievement of our goals and our personal growth.

You probably have a few examples of times in your life when situations first seemed terrible, but now clearly worked out for the best.

A few years ago, we applied for and were rejected for the Renegade Craft Fair 2013 Christmas show. I was **devastated** at the time. We were rejected by the "cool kids." But it was our first Christmas in business, and nothing could have prepared me for the insanity of that first holiday season. I imagined that if we didn't go to the Renegade Craft Fair, our sales would suck and we'd be floundering in obscurity forever.

Blergh!

Instead, **we sold out of everything** well in advance of the Renegade Craft Fair.

If we had been accepted to the show, we would have ended up sitting in folding chairs in the middle of our booth, drinking whiskey and pondering how we just threw away $550 on booth fees for an empty booth.

Not only did everything work out for the best, it worked out in a way that I couldn't have foreseen. My reality didn't include a world where we could sell out of all our products, so I didn't even *think* to hope for that.

# BELL'S PALSY: THE WORST THING FOR THE FRESHMAN YEAR OF HIGH SCHOOL?

Bell's palsy is a condition that freezes the muscles in a person's face. High school, as I'm sure you're aware, is the time when everyone is figuring out pecking order and making judgements about each other. So pretty much, Bell's palsy is one of the most horrifying things that can happen to a teen in freshman year of high school.

But that's how George Clooney spent his formative freshman year.

"It's probably a great thing that it happened to me because it forced me to engage in a series of making fun of myself. And I think that's an important part of being famous. The practical jokes have to be aimed at you," said Clooney of the time, in an interview with Terry Gross on the WHYY/NPR program *Fresh Air*.

George Clooney went on to earn As and Bs in high school—certainly nothing stellar—but his real passion was for baseball and basketball. But in another unfortunate/fortunate twist, he unsuccessfully tried out for the baseball team, the Cincinnati Reds. Having failed at his great love of baseball, he went on to college at Northern Kentucky University, and then University of Cincinnati, but didn't graduate from either.

After that, he made his living selling women's shoes, selling insurance door-to-door, and even cutting tobacco. Certainly nothing glamorous or even related to his current acting, directing, and philanthropic career. But he kept picking up acting gigs—first as an extra, then in a speaking role, then a lead, and now, he also works as a producer. He kept working on his dream, no matter what happened.

George Clooney learned at an early age that these setbacks -- even setbacks as potentially damaging as having a facial muscular problem in high school -- can mean an advantage in life.

In 2009, he was named one of Time Magazine's "Most Influential People in the World." Quite a long way from that freshman kid with the frozen face.

## In every turd pile, there's a seed germinating

Lovely image, right? And sometimes it does feel like pawing through a steaming turd.

The mark of a successful person is how quickly they can set down the ain't-it-awful attitude and find the psychedelic mushroom on the cow patty.

Maybe that's not the right analogy.

But the baseline message is the same: You have to stop feeling sorry for yourself, stop mumbling about how things aren't fair, and start looking for the best possible outcome that you know is hiding in this disappointment somewhere.

And the quicker you can do that, the better off you're going to be. Promise and pinky swear.

## The Pixar formula

Pixar, the animation studio behind such genius movies as *Finding Nemo* and *Up*, has a story formula for their pitches. The formula is:

**1. Once upon a time there was...**

**2. Every day...**

**3. One day...**

**4. Because of that...**

**5. Because of** *that*...

**6. Until finally...**

It's easy to think back to any Pixar movie you've ever seen (and most movies, actually) and see how this story model was applied.

In *Finding Nemo*, the fish were all living together in the sea. Every day, Nemo's dad would take him to school for his lessons. One day, Nemo and his friends got lost and ventured away from the reef. Because of that, they met many other types of fish. Because of *that*, Nemo was caught and trapped in an aquarium. Until finally, he escaped from the aquarium and was reunited with his father.

The major event of Nemo leaving the reef and getting lost caused the entire story to happen. Nemo learned how strong he was, met new friends, and even created a spinoff character, Dory, who went on to have a successful movie franchise of her own. (Some fish get all the breaks, right?)

The thing that has gone "wrong" is an inflection point where a different story—and if you've set your intentions toward positive things, a positive story—is going to unfold.

## THE HOLLYWOOD BLOCK-BUSTED

In his incredible book *The War of Art,* Steven Pressfield talks about his first major Hollywood writing gig: *King Kong Lives.* He wasn't the famous writer he is today, with bestsellers like *The Legend of Bagger Vance* under his belt. He was just a scruffy ol' writer of 42 who had been divorced, rejected, and generally beaten up by life... and then... HOORAH, his big break! He got the opportunity to write *King Kong Lives.*

Pretty huge, right? Huzzah! He had arrived!

He and his co-writer banged out this screenplay that they thought was going to be the *hit movie of the decade*. They saw the finished movie: a **masterpiece**. They rented out the restaurant next to the theater for a huge opening night party... and then, the movie **tanked**. No one saw it. His friends didn't even pretend to say nice things about it to his face. They all scurried away after the movie "like cockroaches," he said.

**A new life thanks to a potentially fatal aneurysm: Ruth—California**

In February 2016, I started experiencing what turned out to be liver toxicity as a result of taking a medication for a very painful nerve condition. At the time, my doctor did not realize

Pressfield was a wreck. He checked the reviews: all awful. He even checked theaters in the suburbs: all awful.

He called his writer friend for sympathy.

His friend said he should be so lucky to be in the arena, instead of the sidelines. Everyone faces failure, he added, and he asked Pressfield if he was going to give up.

Pressfield said he absolutely was NOT going to give up, and he was going to get back to writing immediately!

His friend said, well, that's what the business of being a writer's about! You're taking some knocks, but you're getting back up again! You're in here doing it!

that the medication was the culprit. It would take nearly six months and four neurologists to solve the puzzle, during which my health declined to the point that I could hardly walk unassisted.

My daughter was just about to turn three, I had been married for five and a half years, and my life was in a bit of a rut.

CONT'D. FROM PREVIOUS PAGE...

And because of *that*, Steven Pressfield realized he was a real writer!

He has since written many books, including several about being a professional writer. Those books have gone on to become bestsellers in their own rights, and have encouraged many frustrated writers in their craft, myself included. In fact, it's probably not overstating things to say that if Pressfield's movie hadn't bombed, he might not have written *The War of Art*, and I might not have been able to finish this book.

Aren't you glad *King Kong Lives* tanked? I am!

(If you're a writer, I strongly recommend his books, all of which are listed in the resources section.)

I had found out five years earlier, only six months after we were married, that my husband had been discharged from the Navy for Antisocial Personality Disorder. It took me a while to accept that his explanation of "I was really homesick and took whatever discharge they would give me" was a bunch of malarkey, and he was actually a narcissistic sociopath with odd delusions of grandeur. A non-violent sociopath, thankfully, but a sociopath nonetheless.

Despite thinking to myself almost every day, "this can NOT be the rest of my life," I didn't do anything to change it. Years of emotional abuse and conditioning had me feeling like there was no way I could make it on my own. He wasn't perfect, but at least he was there and providing some sort of financial support, if little else.

In June 2016, I saw Dr. Lizama, a neurologist to whom I was referred by my primary care physician. Originally we were simply going to be looking for alternatives to the medication that I had been taking since January, since I thought something wasn't "right."

Dr. Lizama sent me for an MRI, concerned that the muscle weakness, increased difficulty walking, and hand tremors were indicative of a neurological condition. The radiologist's report came back within a couple of **hours**, and Dr. Lizama's office called me the same day, asking me to schedule an appointment as soon as possible.

They wouldn't discuss the results over the phone. This is the antithesis of "no news is good news."

Dr. Lizama did start with good news, however, when I saw her a few days later. Everything looked good on the MRI in terms of any early signs of Multiple Sclerosis, Parkinson's, or Myasthenia Gravis (she wisely had not told me ahead of time what she was looking for, so I couldn't go home and Google all of those conditions).

Then, oh-so-casually, "The radiologist did, however, find a large aneurysm on your internal carotid artery, just left of center in your brain."

I was in shock at first, and surprisingly calm. Usually when people talk about aneurysms, they're actually talking about ruptured aneurysms, which have a roughly 50/50 chance of being fatal. Of the half that survive, 60% or so have lasting neurological damage.

It wasn't until the day after Dr. Lizama dropped this bombshell that I started looking for the Xanax, feeling like there really was a bomb in my brain that could explode at any time. And we still didn't know what was causing the neurological symptoms! The reason most aneurysms aren't discovered until they leak or rupture is that they don't cause any symptoms, and in the rare cases when they do cause symptoms before rupturing, they're not anything like what I was experiencing.

The first thing I did was apply for a medical leave from my work. I was too weak to continue working 40 hours a week as a shift supervisor at Starbucks, but it was also simply too stressful. Over the next two months I saw three additional neurologists, had a couple more MRIs, a full CT scan of my spine (where I learned I broke my back at some point in the past!), a spinal tap (*super* fun, especially when the doctor hit my spinal cord), and countless blood tests. The doctors were working down an elimination checklist of all the diseases and conditions I **didn't** have, with the exciting final result being Lou Gehrig's Disease (ALS).

The day before I had the nerve conduction test, I remember staring out my kitchen window, and

thinking for the thousandth time, "This can NOT be
the rest of my life."

And that was it. That was the turning point.

I was facing a terminal diagnosis with an average
lifespan of 5 years, and **I had a freaking brain
aneurysm to top it all off**. I decided that if I
really only had a few good years left, I was going
to make them the best they possibly could be, and
that definitely meant making some BIG changes. I
decided I was worthy of being happy.

And then I had the nerve conduction test. And the
neurologist that performed that test happened
to be an expert in Trigeminal Neuralgia, and
as a consequence, was all too familiar with the
liver toxicity, rare though it may be, of the
Carbamazepine I had been taking for nearly 8 months
at that point.

He saw NO indication of ALS, and was more than
mildly surprised that nobody (other than me!) had
thought of stopping the medication. You know, just
to see if that helped. If the nerve pain came back
we would pursue other treatments, but he promised
me that within a week I would feel better, and
within a month I would be back to normal.

I shuffled out of his office, but inside, I was leaping for joy. It felt like I had had my life handed back to me, gift wrapped, with a beautiful bow. By the time I had the brain aneurysm coiled a few weeks later, the only sign of the liver toxicity still hanging around was a slight hand tremor.

Within a month, I asked my husband to move out, and I filed for divorce a month after that. I also started a new job in the midst of all of this—three days after my aneurysm was coiled, to be precise! Joining Outlaw Soaps as their part-time Customer Service Order Fulfillment Manager was originally a bit of a whim, because I didn't want to go back to Starbucks full-time.

A little more than a year after the dust had settled from the not-ALS diagnosis, the aneurysm coiling, and choosing to become a single parent, I was a full-time Outlaw, and had half-jokingly changed my title to Manager of "All Things Outlaw" and am so happy to be a part of this kickass company.

My life isn't perfect, but I am happier on a day-to-day basis than I used to think I had any right to be. "If this isn't nice, I don't know what is."

So many of us just keep trudging along, because it seems too hard, too inconvenient to change things that we know full well are making us unhappy. But the thing is, we only get so many trips 'round the Sun, and none of us know when our ride will be over. We could get a terminal diagnosis tomorrow, we could get hit by a bus crossing the street next week, we could have a brain aneurysm burst. So even if it's hard, or a bit messy, or makes other people look at us like we're a bit crazy (and maybe we are!) life is too short to not do what makes us happy, and eliminate the things that don't. I have a shirt from one of my favorite companies that says: "Life isn't Perfect. Life is Messy. LIFE IS GOOD." The only thing I would add to that sentiment: Life is as good *as we make it*!

1. *Make a list of some disappointing situations that actually turned out for the best. If you struggle to do this, think of any really disappointing situation from more than a year ago and think of what happened to that situation now. Isn't that better?*

2. *Make a list of current fears and worries, and write what you think could be the best possible outcome of each situation.*

3. *Write the next step in making that best possible outcome a reality.*

# day 13: MENTAL ILLNESS IS SO CRAZY

I have spent my entire life riding the waves of mental illness. Many psychiatrists have seen me, and several of them have come to different conclusions. I have treated my mental illness with alcohol and cigarettes. I have been on many medications with many different effects, some positive, and some nearly catastrophic.

fig 2: the worst game ever

This is going to be a very short chapter because, even with all my personal experience in and out of mental illness, I am still unqualified to provide guidance... except this: Get Help.

My experience of mental illness can change how I feel about a day completely independent of what happens on that day. I could win the lottery, but if I won the lottery on a "bad day," I would still be suffocating in depression. More often than not, it has nothing to do with situations, and everything to

do with the weird kaleidoscope of filters I am looking at the world through.

## It's not about the situation

Years ago, in my vast struggles to correct whatever's wrong with my head, I read a book called *Plato, not Prozac*. In it, Lou Marinoff explains that depression is really only how we feel when we're not living a life in accordance with our core values.

Marinoff, in long, disparaging monologues against traditional mental health care, claims that mental health doesn't have anything to do with what traditional counselors and psychologists want you, their customer, to "work through." He says it's about your life philosophy. If you're not living in accordance with your core life philosophy, you're going to be depressed. Marinoff then puts forth several life philosophies based on the work of past philosophers in hopes that the reader will find one and change his or her life to be more aligned.

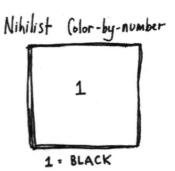

I chose Nihilism: Life is meaningless, we are meaningless. Everything is dust, it returns to dust. It is all dust. Who the fuck cares?

So, yeah, my life philosophy and my daily life mirrored each other pretty perfectly, but it didn't exactly make me feel less depressed.

I have clinical mental health issues, and my mental health issues will color every life philosophy I choose. Untreated, it will make me (and anyone else suffering from mental illness) fold inward infinitely until there's nowhere left to fold. At which point, we mental illness sufferers often die.

"Mental health," to people like Marinoff, is a concept invented by pharmaceutical companies trying to sell stuff, not trying to make life better for people.

"Patient, heal thyself!" It is an irresponsible attitude that I think poses a real life-or-death danger to people who have unbalanced brain chemistry.

"Just go for a walk!"

"Have you tried meditation?"

"Yoga really puts me in a better headspace. You should try it!"

It is impossible to explain to someone who isn't suffering from depression how upsetting these suggestions are. At once, they minimize the importance of what we, the depressed person, are trying to share ("I feel like dying. No, really, I feel like I should die."), and they close off an opportunity to address the root of the depression: faulty brain chemicals.

New research suggests that depression could actually be an inflammation reaction. This was celebrated and shared by depression-sufferers everywhere, because it confirms what we have been trying to say all along: "There is actually something broken in my brain." And if that broken thing is an allergic reaction, non-depressed people might finally understand how real it is.

## You *can* feel better

About six years ago, I was so depressed that I couldn't get my head right for weeks. Before that, I had tried to kill myself on a few occasions. I have mental health issues.

A couple days ago, I was so depressed I decided to take a mental health day—which turned into a mental health couple-hours. I went to bed, slept for a bit, cried some, and felt a little better, and went back to work. I have successfully learned to manage my depression. This doesn't mean I don't have depression, but it is no longer running my life.

It is possible to feel better. I am living proof.

First, understand that it's not about some philosophical stance on medication, or how you "should be able to be fine" without medication. If you have been born with the disability of having brain chemistry that is amiss, your pragmatic attitude about pharmaceuticals is as misplaced as an asthmatic gasping for air and pushing away inhalers.

*Am I saying the pharmaceutical industry isn't trying to make a buck off you? No. I think they probably are, and with varying degrees of ethics. But if you're resisting treatment because you have something philosophical against drug companies, you're only hurting yourself. If you have depression, you need treatment.*

Second, one drug is not the same as another. I have gone through many kinds of treatment before finding the combination that works to keep me above water. You might have bad effects from one medication, which is why it's important to see a doctor regularly until you get your mental health on an even keel.

Third, drugs are best used in concert with a focused effort to improve the situational stressors in your life. Marinoff was right about one thing: just treating depression with drugs isn't going to be as successful as taking a look at your life and making sure you're on a path of situational improvement. If you're so broke you can't take your cat to the vet, it's going to be very hard to feel super positive about life.

Fourth, if nothing is working, you aren't a hopeless case, you haven't failed, this isn't a life sentence of sadness. Just keep going. The only failure is the failure to keep going.

Fifth, and finally, sometimes you have to just ride things out. Realizing that I could acknowledge my feelings and also acknowledge that they will change was a massive life improvement. Yes, everything awful seems to happen on the same day for absolutely no reason. I don't understand it either. But knowing that in three days, the situational nightmare will be over, and I'll still be standing... there's power in that.

My doctor recommended the book *Feeling Good* by David Burns, and I have found it to be the best non-medical treatment for my depression. It is a very long book, and my doctor only recommended the first part, so that's what I'm recommending to you.

I hope you get relief from this legitimate issue. You are worth it.

## HYPERBOLE AND A HALF

Allie Brosh had one of the most popular blogs on the internet. She wrote about her life's events and non-events, illustrated with primitive and colorful cartoons drawn in PC Paint. Over the years, her blog acquired a following of thousands of dedicated readers.

And then she vanished.

Months went by without a new post, and those of us who were loyal readers got pretty worried.

In a sudden spill of posts, Brosh returned with some painfully real, honest stories about her deep depression. She shared about her youth growing up with depression, about how she felt: sad, then awful, then lost, and then... nothing. And how finally, when she felt nothing, she felt like she could do anything.

Her posts were the most real and accurate portrayal of depression I had ever seen, and they got millions of views. My family shared them around. They opened up conversations around depression that had previously been shallow and misunderstood.

And then she vanished again.

And then one post came out: she was writing a book. That post got 1.5 million pageviews on its first day online. She was surprised people even remembered her.

On her book tour, she talked about her depression. It resonated so deeply with people—many who felt very alone in their struggle—and Brosh let them know they weren't alone.

She still struggles with depression. I know this because she hasn't posted in a long time. Her voice and perspective is missed.

ACTION STEP:

*If you have mental health concerns, your action step is to make an appointment with a psychiatrist. If you don't know of a psychiatrist, call your doctor's office and ask for a recommendation. If you don't have a doctor or don't want to call yours, you can find one on* **therapists.psychologytoday.com/ rms** *or* **www.thero.org.** *Many of them accept* *various forms of insurance, so you may be able to see one for free, on a sliding scale (where you pay what you can afford), or for a low copay.*

If you do not have mental health concerns, or you're already being treated for mental health (congratulations!), you get a free day!

**DAY 14**

# WEEK in REVIEW

This week, we did some heavy duty work (haha, I said "duty") on the bug-infested under-rock areas. You might be feeling a little tender right now. Personally, I get a little scared and oogie when I see all my weird and uncomfortable fears and beliefs right there in my journal.

So today, practice some self-love. Whether that's just a full day of mindless vegging out on the couch, some time out in nature, a hot bath, or an early night to bed, just go ahead and treat yourself.

You're amazing. You really have gone through a lot—not just this week, but through it all, through everything.

If you need some ideas of fun self-love, visit danielleavincent.com/selflove.

Part 3:
OTHER PEOPLE

# Forgiveness Part 1: Forgiving others

*"Holding onto anger is like drinking poison and expecting the other person to die."*

— ANONYMOUS

This book is all about *useful and practical stuff*, so I wouldn't put you through this if it wasn't important.

When someone transgresses on our values, we get angry and hurt. That's helpful, because it gives us a moral and ethical line in the sand. We know where our values are, and unfortunately, where the transgressor's values are not.

OSS ETHICAL LINE DO NOT CROSS ETI

We get to make decisions about our own values based on our reaction: for example, if someone cheats on us, and we are hurt, that means we value monogamy. It also means that they don't value monogamy (at least as much as we hoped they did). And often, that signifies a divergence in values vast enough to justify the end of a relationship.

Grudges are there to protect us from ever getting hurt in that way again. They serve a purpose, and like all our other quirks, we have to give them a lot of credit.

When you refuse to forgive someone, and when you hold on to anger, it often feels like you are upholding a moral or ethical standard. That person did that thing and you refuse to accept it. And in order to hold up that moral or ethical standard, you feel like you have to hold on to that anger against the person.

But you can still uphold that standard without keeping the poison of a grudge in your life. Your values are no longer any of their business and nothing they did has anything to do with you upholding your values. And you can also decide never to see them again or have anything to do with them. Or you can continue to have a pleasant familial relationship with them, and also decide not to extend the relationship outside the bounds of those particular situations.

Your standards don't have to have anything to do with their behavior.

People have asked me about this chapter: "Does this mean I have to have them back in my life?" H-E-double-hockey-sticks to the no. I wouldn't do that to you. You are the sole determinator of who is in your life and who's out.

All I'm sayin' is that you have to go through the process of figuring out the value from the transgression (you learned about yourself and you learned about them), and you have to forgive them.

## You have to figure out who you're mad at and forgive them

If you immediately thought, "Ok, sure, but *not my ex-boyfriend Carl.* To Hell with that guy," welcome to probably one of the hardest exercises in the book.

Before you put down this book and walk away: You don't have to forgive them to their face, you don't have to get involved in their quicksand-life, you don't have to forget what they've done, and you don't have to even tell them you're forgiving them.

This is *just for you.*

See, no progress is possible as long as you're holding a grudge. You'll encounter blocks to your financial security in *seriously crazy ways* that aren't even rational. You'll be turned down for promotions that are rightfully yours. The resentments will spiral and build into a huge, steaming pile of doo right on top of your heart. Everyone will smell it and be repelled.

Oh God, it's so awful.

And yet, sometimes **not** forgiving someone for something *truly unforgivable* feels better than rinsing off your ol' doo-doo heart. It feels solid and good to have a real good reason to hate someone. It defines "right" and "wrong" to us. It draws the line in the sand about what we think is acceptable and what is **not acceptable**.

You'll never hear from me that having ethical boundaries is wrong.

But that person (and that person's actions) have nothing to do with *your* ethical boundaries. They don't have the same ethical boundaries (or if they do, they crossed them). They did what they did, and now you gotta do what you gotta do.

And you gotta forgive them.

## What are our values here?

You know how I said that the good thing about having someone transgressing on our values is that we learn more about us and our values? And yeah, of course we're mad, but we're going to do what we can to suck every life lesson out of this, and values is a pretty huge and awesome lesson.

Why are you mad at the person? What did they do that was hard to forgive?

At first, you'll probably vomit a bunch of stuff that seems obvious: SHE SERIOUSLY STOLE MONEY FROM ME! WHEN I WAS HER ROOMMATE!

Ok, pretty bad, right?

From this, we can pull that we value money. But really, it's not so much the money that's the issue. If she stole our car, we'd be pretty upset too, right? Yes. Ok, cookin' with gas.

So we value not stealing. And kiiiiinnnd of everyone believes that, right? Well, I stole a napkin from a restaurant once because it was this super hilarious checker pattern and I was drunk.*So, is it a size of stealing issue? If she stole $2.50, maybe the approximate value of the napkin, would I still be mad?

Yes, I definitely would. But probably not "ending friendship or doubting her entire value as a human" mad. So I'm mad that she stole a fairly large amount of money from me. Yes, I think it's important when other people respect my property, in amounts over, say, $40?

Well, I guess I'd need a damn good explanation. So, if they had a *really good reason*, and they weren't just stealing it for convenience.

It turns out, we have quite a lot of values we can investigate around this, ya know?

I think prior behavior probably factors into it, so if I trusted her, and it was a significant amount of money, and it was for something frivolous, the problem gets bigger and bigger.

So my values are:
· Being trustworthy
· Respecting my property around important things
· Having a sense of relative importance that is aligned with mine

*Yes, this is true. I still have that napkin in my "box of stuff I have so many amazing memories around," because I was on a vacation with a friend of mine and we took almost no pictures, and that napkin is one of the only mementos from that trip.

136    And yes, I am ashamed. Stealing is wrong in any amount, under any circumstances.

And that is something super helpful I can take with me to future relationships. If I ever decide to communicate with the person in question about this incident again, I'll have a very clear set of values to express and be able to identify exactly how my values were violated, which hopefully turns this into a teachable—if not entirely kumbaya—moment.

## Why forgiveness

I don't claim to know how it works, all I know is that *it works*.

When I first discovered the Angry Person's Forgiveness Method (below), I was working as hard as I could on my financial stability. For my entire life, I have struggled with financial security (or lack thereof), and I was getting pretty damn desperate to have some security. I couldn't figure out what the hell was wrong with me that I couldn't manage to hold on to *literally any* amount of money.

I made six figures a year for many, many years and had nothing to show for it (ok, I did have some really fantastic shoes and a lot of adventures to show for it, but nothing saved for my lean years). I already talked about it back in "Day 9: It's all in your mind," so I won't dive back into the details here, but for me, financial stability was a mental block, so even though I knew how to keep a budget, I just **couldn't**.

I had to hide money from myself (no, really, I have sent my friend Teresa thousands of dollars for her to save me from myself). If money wasn't nailed down, I'd spend it.

But I got serious about fixing my financial issues (see the resources section at the end for some books I recommend), and so was trying *anything* to fix these mental blocks.

On a long road trip, where I was listening to *The 4 Spiritual Laws of Prosperity*, the author said that she tooth-grittingly forgave everyone, including her no good, low down, cheatin' ex-husband.

"Tooth-gritting?" That didn't sound very clean or magical to me.

But if that was all that was required, I was going to give it a shot. So on that long drive, I turned off the book and started yelling at the top of my lungs all the people I had to forgive, and that I forgave them, and what I forgave them for.

Which is how I invented...

## The angry person's forgiveness

*Sigh.* Look, I want to tell you that you should just let the spirit of love and generosity into your heart, which will magically wash away the anger. But I'm not a fricken' fairy godmother, and I know that forgiveness doesn't work that way for me, so let's just assume it doesn't work that way for you either. Especially for the particularly sticky wickets, yaknowwhatI'msayin'?

In your mind, you probably have a buried rolodex (or maybe it's a spreadsheet... I don't know your brain) of people who have wronged you. In the car,

I sure checked in with my internal rolodex of people who had done me wrong.

Mine was easy to start...

"MARLA, I FORGIVE YOU FOR STEALING FROM ME WHEN YOU WERE MY ROOMMATE. I FORGIVE YOU. SETH, I FORGIVE YOU FOR SAYING YOU LOVED ME AND THEN DUMPING ME AFTER I MOVED ALL THE WAY TO A DIFFERENT CITY FOR YOU! I FORGIVE YOU! SAM, I FORGIVE YOU FOR DRINKING ON THAT CAMP-ING TRIP WHEN YOU PROMISED YOU'D SUPPORT ME IN MY SOBRIETY. I FORGIVE YOU!"

I yelled it out one by one, for every person I could think of, throughout my whole life.

"KRISTEN, I FORGIVE YOU FOR HOOKING UP WITH MY EX-BOYFRIEND EVEN THOUGH I ASKED YOU NOT TO. I FORGIVE YOU!"

If I still felt mad, I yelled it again a few times just for good measure until I felt less mad.

Every disappointment, every betrayal, every violation of trust... I unloaded as much as I could into the void of my car on that one road trip. Throughout the rest of the trip, whenever something would come into my head that I was still mad about, I'd stop the audiobook and yell into the car a few times.

There are lots of exercises about forgiveness, about seeing the other person's perspective, about making peace with them... and I'm sure those are all **better** than this method. I'm sure they're more cleansing and more thorough.

If you feel like you *can* smooth over the wrinkles in your heart with some more graceful solutions, by all means, do it. But if you can't quite get to that point, just yell your forgiveness in the car at the top of your lungs. It does still work.

And did it work for me? Absolutely.

I now have an *actual savings account* where I had none. We have some degree of financial security, and then we got a massive loan for our business, which helped us to build an even better business.

I don't claim to know how all this works (let's go back to that part about suspending your disbelief), but it really does work. Whether it's your finances, your health, your hobbies and interests, your community, or your mate, you have to forgive people before you can manifest the awesome stuff awaiting you.

Forgiveness works. However you gotta get it done.

1. *Write a list of people who you should forgive—no matter how large or small the offense—in your notebook (add to this as necessary).*

2. *Wherever is appropriate (probably not in your workplace open floor plan), yell out forgiveness to them as many times as you need to in order to feel less angry.*

## People are doing the best they can

I was reading Brené Brown's book *Rising Strong* (which I totally recommend), and in it, she explores a thought that she took for granted, but was surprised to find that not everyone agreed with.

She felt like everyone was *not* doing the best they can all the time.

When I heard this, I was upset. And then I was confused. Surely the queen of heart-centered and research-driven introspection *had to believe* that everyone is doing the best they can.

I asked my therapist in our next session: "Do you think people are doing the best they can?"

She replied, incredulous: "Absolutely not. What, do you?"

I said: "Yes, I absolutely believe they are."

Ok, so here are two mental health professionals in agreement that people are not doing the best they can. And me, incurable optimist (apparently), completely off-base about other people's intentions.

But here's the thing: I know I have done really disappointing things. Even as recently as last weekend, I forgot that my friend was coming to stop by on her way back from Burning Man, and instead of staying home to meet her, I booked a flight to Los Angeles to work on the book. I *totally* forgot. I apologized. I do feel awful.

But I also know that I was doing the absolute best I could, given everything that's going on, our business, the book, and my contract work. I just can't keep everything in mind.

And I think that's the case for everyone. Everyone really is just doing the shittiest best they can, even if they're shitheads.

And then also, later in the chapter, Brené came around and decided that people are, in fact, generally doing the best they can. VINDICATED! Did I ever say I wasn't petty? No, I did not.

Ultimately, we don't know how people were raised or what tools they were given to handle all of life's circumstances. Heck, we don't even know *our own* faulty tool kits. People are being driven by generations of messed up stuff. And we don't have to voluntarily put *ourselves* in harm's way of all that messed up stuff, but at least maybe it explains a little of it.

## Road rage

While we're on the subject of yelling in cars, I want to talk a little about bad drivers. They're out there, cutting you off, not paying attention, being assholes, and then suddenly they're in the driver's seat of your fricken' day. You think about them once you get out of the car, you walk around with their stupid honk right over your shoulder, and you carry their mindless careening around the office with you.

This is just ridiculous, my friend.

*They're* not walking around with it inside them all day (probably), so why should *you*? You'll never see them again (hopefully), and why let them take over what would otherwise be a pretty fine day?

In the car, instead of yelling whatever else you'd yell at them, just yell "I FORGIVE YOU, DOUCHEBAG WHO CUT ME OFF WITHOUT USING YOUR STUPID SIGNAL. I FORGIVE YOU." Or, you know, whatever the applicable situation is.

# Forgiveness Part 2: Forgive yourself

## Sometimes it's harder to forgive ourselves than it is to forgive others.

I n fact, it has taken me longer to write this chapter than any other chapter in this book, because not only is the act of forgiveness really hard, even the act working up to the act is hard, and even *looking at the act* is hard.

This is because not only do we have to forgive ourselves for things we have done that harm other people—often people we love today, and often things they don't even know about—we have to forgive ourselves for generally not measuring up to our own expectations of what it means to be a "good person."

It's *huge*.

And also, it's totally impossible.

Which is why it has taken me dang near forever to write this chapter. How do I describe something so huge that it is literally impossible and takes an entire lifetime, and perhaps more?

WAKE UP
KICK ASS
REPEAT

But it's 6am and I have a cup of coffee in a cup that says "Wake up. Kick ass. Repeat." So I'm gonna go for it.

## At the most basic level, forgiveness is just compassion

I tried using the Angry Person's Forgiveness Method on myself and yelling at myself doesn't really have the intended result. So, you can go ahead and give it a try, but it didn't work for me.

Whatever we do wrong, whether it's being a bad friend to someone else, or being a bad friend to ourselves, we fail to measure up to our expectations. We are disappointed in ourselves, and we might start to categorize ourself as a "bad person" (see earlier chapter about not being one thing). Over our lifetimes, because we are human and being a human is kind of a zoo, we disappoint ourselves over and over. It's pretty easy to work up enough evidence that we are "bad people" over our lifetimes.

But no person is perfect. Part of being alive is making mistakes, acting badly, and recovering. We are driven by conflicting hopes, expectations, and desires, and these conflicts cause us to act in ways that are imperfect.

As long as we are going through life, we are making mistakes. Sometimes they're only mistakes we can see in retrospect, when the unintended consequence hurts someone we love. And we feel disappointed with our lack of foresight, with our selfish behavior, with ourselves.

And yeah, that sucks.

We fail to measure up to our expectations. We fall short. We disappoint ourselves. We feel awful about it.

But that's how we learn and grow. That is how we become better people. That is how we take a real look at what it means to be a good person. It's part of the whole experience, and the person who doesn't make mistakes, who doesn't hurt, and who doesn't have to forgive themselves isn't really living.

To forgive ourselves, we have to take a real look at the things we have done, both to ourselves and to others, and intentionally go down the list and think of the lesson that came from each experience. We have to thank that experience for teaching us the lesson. And we have to forgive ourselves.

## Residual self-forgiveness

AND EVEN AFTER THAT, you might still have some residual non-forgiveness that comes up in echoes. You'll be driving down the street, and all of a sudden, you'll think "OMG I CAN'T BELIEVE I COULD BE SO STUPID."

In that moment, you have to compassionately say (out loud or to yourself), "I forgive myself. I am grateful for what I

learned. I forgive myself."

## It's a mess

The whole thing is a mess, which is why it took me a hundred years to write this chapter. The truth is, I still suck at forgiving myself.

In all my years of research, I haven't found any truly "easy" methods for forgiving people—either yourself or others. I think it's just a mess for everyone. In order to write this chapter, I had to forgive myself for struggling to forgive myself, which was a real into-the-mirror experience.

But I'm a human. And all I can do is bring my best to this moment, which is the best any of us can hope for.

ACTION STEPS:

*1. Write down the things you need to forgive yourself for. It won't be an exhaustive list, but take 5 - 10 minutes or so on this part of the action step anyways.*

*2. For each item, make a note of what you learned from that experience.*

*3. For each item, read it over, and say "I forgive myself for _____."*

# How to lose friends and ignore people

I t has been said that you are the average of the five people you spend the most time with. Does that give you pause? Are you surrounded by awesome people you're striving to be more like, or bitter, sad, angry complainers?

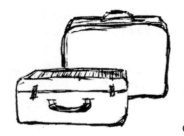

Most people have a mix of friends on a range of levels, and that's good, because it means that not only do we have people who elevate us, we also have people who deserve our compassion, because they're really struggling.

Just like you need to take care of your own mask on an airplane before helping those around you, you have to stay solid in your own development (especially during this month) before worrying about the development of others.

Some people are going through legitimately hard times, and part of being a good friend is being their friends through this. In Day 18, we'll talk about how to be a good friend. But right now, today, for this exercise, we're going to focus on our own masks.

I have found one or two people *immediately* come to mind when I mention "chronic complainers" who are "bitter, sad, and angry all the time." These are the people we're going to take a little vacation from.

## Contagious worldviews: when other people's baggage starts rubbing off on you

Being friends with someone usually means carrying around a lot of their baggage. This is because the way they see and relate to the world is transferred to you as "their experience."

For example, your friend is recounting an experience at a restaurant where the server was incredibly rude. But was the server actually rude? If you were in that restaurant observing the same things, would you have observed a completely different situation? Would you have noticed that the server was on the verge of crying, and so was trying to leave the table quickly so as not to start crying at the table? Would you have noticed that your friend's kid had thrown pudding at the server's skirt while your friend wasn't looking? Would the tone of the server not even have come across as rude to you, if you were in that same situation at that same time?

Your friend's baggage—the whole way your friend frames life—is being conveyed to you in the recounting of this, and every, story. No one is an infallible witness. Even the editorial choice of stories to share transmits and reinforces a worldview... which then becomes *your* worldview.

If your friend believes that people are basically bad people, the stories your friend tells you are going to support that belief for you. And in that way, your friend's baggage is going to rub off on you.

This goes *especially* for the largely-unfiltered world of social media, where people are just a nonstop fountain of personal worldviews.

*Side note: This works both ways. If you're recounting stories to your friends, think about what worldview you are reinforcing for them. Are you enhancing their life or deteriorating it?*

Hopefully you can see how important it is to be *very mindful* of the company you keep.

## Getting rid of people gently, without getting involved in their stuff

I used to make a big deal out of "sharing" with people why I couldn't be friends with them anymore. I thought this could help them in some way, like they'd suddenly snap out of their sad lives and have a mega "ah-ha" moment, and then we could be bosom buddies.

Or alternatively, sometimes I'd "share" that I was going through a personal development as a passive aggressive way of telling them that I was mad at them or that I felt hurt by their actions. I'd say that I was seeking closure, wrapping up loose ends, and giving them "the explanation they deserved."

I've come to realize that all that is just a lot of extra work and bad feelings that no one—not you or them—needs.

I know this may sound hard to do, but you're gonna have to trust me: just let them go. For this month. And then you can decide what to do after that. Say you're busy, say you're working on a project (which is true—*you're* kind of a project now!), or say that you're focusing on trying to sort out your goals and dreams.

Whatever. It doesn't really matter. What matters is that you're giving yourself space from that worldview while you develop your own newer, fresher, more productive and awesome worldview.

## Keep the rockstars

Which of your friends passes the "supportive, awesome, positive" test? It's sometimes hard to really see clearly. If you're like me, you've accumulated friends, and friendships have changed over time.

We're not looking to cut out your best friend from high school, but we are looking to see if we can identify and elevate the people who should get the priority of your time. Time is valuable, so you want to be sure to make the space for people who are awesome, while quietly letting the others adrift.

## Let the rockstars in!!

If you honestly look around and think "eesh, *all* the people I hang out with are kind of cranky, bitchy, mean, bitter people," you're going to need some new friends. It might seem like having friends is better than being alone, but once you cut out the non-helpful people, you'll be surprised and delighted by how many amazing people start entering your life.

We're going to talk more about finding and keeping your team tomorrow.

**ACTION STEP:**

*On the next pages are 10 qualities that we want to increase in our lives. Think of friends who embody these qualities—really just the first person or people that come to mind when you read it—and write their name(s) down next to the item. If you can't think of anyone, leave that cell blank and make a mental note to find people who fit that quality. In the next chapter, we'll talk about how to bring more awesome people into your life.*

You can download a printable version of this chart at **you-nicorn.com/day17**

| Supportive of me pursuing my highest goals | |
| --- | --- |
| Makes and encourages healthy lifestyle choices | |
| Listens when I want to talk | |
| Handles problems and challenging situations in healthy, productive ways | |
| Laughs easily, warmly | |
| Is trustworthy and has integrity | |
| Embodies qualities I would like to possess | |

| Respects my time and interests | |
| --- | --- |
| Offers words of encouragement, rather than just sympathy, when I'm feeling low | |
| Is kind to strangers (particularly service staff) | |

# Cultivating healthy friendships with people who believe in you

## Focus on your team

Please whip out your notebook and revisit yesterday's chart, because we're going to find your cheer squad.

See who you identified as someone who is "Supportive of me pursuing my highest goals" and for the superstars in the "Handles problems and challenging situations in healthy, productive ways" department. These people are gonna be your dream team, and we're going to cultivate super special friendships with them.

Look at the list of qualities that make up a "positive" friend (the grid in the last chapter). Would you show up in this list for your friends? Do you believe in your friends and do you let them know, in no uncertain terms, exactly how amazing you think they are? Do you offer positive solutions to problems (when they ask)? Do you offer enthusiastic words of encouragement and positivity, or are you a co-miserator?

Resolve to do more of the things that make up supportive, positive friendships for the people who you're fond of. These people **already deserve your enthusiastic praise and support**, so it should be easy to just offer words of praise and support in passing.

At this point, don't worry about being a great friend for people who are in the "ain't it awful" club. You're mostly not spending time with them anyways, right?

## Keeping and cultivating good friendships

In order to keep good friendships good, we have to honor and respect those friendships. And we *should* honor and respect good friendships, because good friends are hard to find.

I'm assuming that you're pretty familiar with the basic tenets of friendship:

**1: Treat the other person like you'd want to be treated (e.g., don't sleep with their partner or whatever)**

**2: Make time for the other person (and don't flake out or be chronically late)**

**3: Listen and empathize when they want to talk about an issue**

**4: Be kind**

But there are some confusing elements that come up from time to time, too. What if your friend complains about stuff? A lot? What if your friend used to be super positive, but recently is going through some hard times? Do you just take a hard-line "GOOD VIBES ONLY" stance?

You have to be compassionate. Yeah, we're all responsible for the situations in our lives, but we also have to have compassion for the traumas people are going through. Remember how hard Day 2's exercise was? Everyone has their Day 2 and to have a friend, you have to be a friend.

There's a big difference between eliminating negativity and being an asshole. Please always act compassionately. Protect yourself, but be compassionate.

## Time & friendships

I'm going to share a story that I'm not particularly proud of. A few years ago, we were just starting our business and it was really overwhelming me. I didn't have my life together at all, and yet I really wanted to hang out with my friend Megan*.

Megan is not just a fantastic person, she's an incredible esthetician. Her schedule is always full—usually more than full—with people lining up to hand her money.

Because she loves me, though, she's always willing to make time for me if I want to see her.

During this particularly challenging period, I made two dates with her, and flaked out twice.

"Danielle," she called me after I texted saying I couldn't make it the second time, "I have to respect my time. I need *you* to respect my time. I didn't take clients this morning because I thought we were going to hang out. So until you can make a commitment to respect my time, I can't schedule anything with you. I still love you, but I need you to figure out when you really can commit, and we can schedule something for then."

Ow, right? Ow.

But she was totally right, and I was grateful that she drew that boundary.

I have been various degrees of flaky throughout my life, but since then, I have really tried to only make plans when I am 100% sure I can show up, or I have managed the expectations of the person I'm making plans with. If I might be tired, I will sometimes qualify plans with, "I'm making plans, but I don't know how up for it I'll feel. Is that ok?" Sometimes that's ok, and sometimes it isn't, and I'm glad I know in advance.

I got the boundaries drawn, and I'm passing it along to you so you don't have to. Friendship means respecting someone's time and expectations. Period.

So.... with all that in mind, are you ready to be a great friend?

## Finding friends

> "The only way to have a friend is to be one."
>
> –UNKNOWN

About 30 years ago, when I had no friends, I picked up a little card with this quote. I stuck it on the back of my bedroom door, hoping it would somehow magically change my life and generate a friend.

A little back story... When I was about 7 years old, I transferred from public school in Boston to private school in Seattle. Our class of about 40 students were of a higher economic caste than I was, wore fashionable clothes, and had known each other since kindergarten. To use a cultural analogy, they were Ralph Lauren, and I was Mossimo for Target.

We had absolutely *nothing* in common. I was physically awkward since my limbs grew about twice as fast as my torso. My sports skills were nonexistent and much of popularity in that school was based on athletics. I was a quiet, bookish kid with a bowl cut hairdo. I had braces. On top of all that, I only much later was diagnosed with Asperger Syndrome, so I struggled to relate to other kids. I didn't pick up on social standards (I'll go into that part later).

I mention all this now, not because I want to get sympathy, but because I think it's important to note where I am coming from when I say that I know it's hard to find friends.

*The Ugly Duckling* is the story of my life.

In case you're not familiar with the story, *The Ugly Duckling* is about a family of ducks in a pond. One duckling was *so ugly*, awkward, and different that all the other ducklings teased him ruthlessly. Ducks can be *so cruel.* But eventually, they went to a bigger part of the pond, and the ugly duckling saw some other ducklings that looked like him... but they weren't ducklings, they were *swans.* The duckling was super ugly, gray, and runty because it was actually a swan chick.

There are some problems with the story. I don't know why the mom duck took this runty chick that must have come from a different looking egg, but let's gloss over the obvious plot holes in this children's book. The moral of the story is that once an oddball duck gets into a bigger pond, he or she will find other oddball ducks like them, and they won't be oddballs anymore.

As soon as I entered the larger world, I was able to find my tribe.

Since you're reading this in the age of the internet, your tribe has never been closer and easier to find. If you find yourself in a vacuum of community, your swan brethren and sisteren are out there.

I have found some of my strongest support teams in online self-help courses. You may want to enroll in our

YOU-NICORN coaching group (free) so you can be surrounded by positive people who are on an enthusiastic trajectory!

Heck, we even have an online group called "Masters of our Fate, Captains of our Soul." You can access the group by going to my website: danielleavincent.com/community

ACTION STEPS:

1. Go back to the friend list from the last chapter and reach out to some of the people on the list. Make a date with these people, whether it's in person, by video, or on the phone. Just catch up and chat!

2. If you're a real fan of theirs, and feeling generous, you might want to get them on the same vibe plan as you by sending them this book. YOU see the YOU-UNICORN in them, so they probably could benefit from the book too, right?

3. *Let them know that you appreciate them and their enthusiasm. It won't be weird, I promise. Just drop them a quick note, text, email, or talk to them in human voice talking conversations (people do this still, right?) to let them know that you know they've always believed in you, expected the best of you, and that you really appreciate it. You don't have to give them any examples (or you might want to if one comes to mind), but it's important to let them know that it's meaningful to you.*

What we tend to grows, so we want to make sure they feel tended to.

# day 19:
# PEOPLE WANT TO HELP YOU

I n this mad, mad world, it's easy to start to see everyone else—namely strangers, work colleagues, and/or family—as either neutral or negative forces in the achievement of our goals. In truth, the opposite is true. People want to help you. Even strangers. Even that cantankerous co-worker who you swear is giving you the evil eye when you speak up at meetings.

Part of this is just plain old mundane truth: people are generally helpful. But part of it has to do with the work you're already doing in this book: once you start setting your sights on your highest ambitions and hopes, The Universe does conspire to help you.

I promised you this book wouldn't be too woo-woo, so you don't have to take my word for it if you don't want to believe right now. But there will be a day when the evidence is just too overwhelming to ignore.

"Don't try to understand! It's enough if you do not misunderstand."

—NISARADATTA MAHARAJ

163

When we show we're making improvements in our lives (as you're doing), people help us in surprising and magical ways. People who we haven't talked to in years suddenly re-enter our lives, a stranger at the gas station says just the right thing in just the right way, we are introduced to someone at a party who happens to work where we wanted to get a job!

Watch for these coincidences and connections, because they're pretty magic.

## AMANDA PALMER - PERFORMANCE ARTIST & MUSICIAN

One of Amanda Palmer's first jobs was standing on a crate dressed as a bride, waiting for people to put money in her hat. She asked. People gave. There was a symbiotic relationship which she felt created a profound connection between herself and the giver.

She also was in a relatively unknown band called The Dresden Dolls. As the band got more popular and started touring, she left her "8 foot bride" position and started a different kind of asking: performing, stage-diving, and generally letting her audience catch her, both literally and figuratively.

At one show, a fan ran up and handed her a $10 bill. He said that he had ripped her album, but wanted to make sure she got paid

# People want to help you at work

One of the notes I have stuck to every computer that I could possibly write email/take meetings/communicate with others on is "People want to help you." This reminds me that no matter what it looks like, people are actively trying to help me.

for her work, and the contribution she had made to his life.

She describes this as the turning point in her life, where she realized that she didn't have to force people to pay her for her work, she could just ask them, and they would voluntarily contribute. She doesn't want to hold her music hostage anymore.

Such was born "The Art of Asking," which was a life philosophy, then a TED Talk, and eventually a book.

Palmer found that her fans were so enthusiastic about supporting her work, that they gave more than $1.2 million through Kickstarter to create a new album. She now freely gives away her music, and is supported by her fans.

When I worked at Oprah, there were a lot of office politics that got me down. My direct manager was a truly excellent person (and a friend to this day), but she inserted herself into nearly every one of my projects and made decisions without informing me. I felt that she was trying to undermine my projects, and maybe even take credit (which I didn't really care about, I just wanted to be sure the project was a success). At the very least, I was sure it *definitely* meant that she didn't believe I was qualified enough to take care of the project myself.

When I started at Mozilla as a contractor, a couple people started setting up meetings to "give extra hands" and "help out." I had flashbacks and was *sure* they were trying to take over my projects because they felt I was incompetent or unfit to run the projects. My insecurities were high. I went directly to my boss and explained the situation. "Oh sure, they're just helping."

I realized with an unpleasant "OMG WHAT HAVE I DONE?" feeling that I had been assuming the worst of people, when really, people were trying to *help me.*

I pondered all the times when I had thought people didn't like me or were trying to subtly get into my projects, and with great horror, I realized how much **better** and **easier** my life would have been if I just assumed people were trying to help me.

Since then, I stuck stickers all over everything I could in order to remind myself that, paranoia be damned, people *are trying to help me.*

# It's ok to ask. Heck, you might as well ask!

In the last few years, I have discovered the magic of just asking. Really, it's *wild*. It turns out that not only do people *want* to help you! But most of the time, they aren't sure how exactly to help. So when you ask, you're *doing them the favor* of letting them know what you need.

Think of how good you feel when you do something nice for someone else. Especially when you know that person to be a wonderful individual. Don't you feel great? Don't you feel like you're walking on a ray of sun? And if the person is super appreciative, don't you feel closer to them? Don't you feel like you have a new bond to them? No, not that they "owe you" something, but just that you have something that you shared.

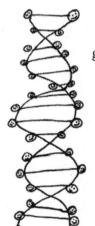

People *love* helping. Really, they do. I don't know what's in our DNA that makes us feel good when we help other people.

Give it a try today: ask for something that you want. It doesn't have to be super huge, just ask a small favor.

## Gratitude makes the whole thing go 'round

When someone helps, we have to thank them from our heart. Not just to their face (which is very important), but in a way that blesses them—kind of like whispering goodness into The Universe's ear. We have to be grateful for the smallest

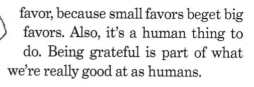

favor, because small favors beget big favors. Also, it's a human thing to do. Being grateful is part of what we're really good at as humans.

So when someone helps you, express gratitude and internalize gratitude.

## Ok, but the truth is...

A friend/co-worker who saw one of my notes laughed and said, "But that's not true. Not always, at least." And ok, I have to admit that there are some people who are just real assholes—or at least they're more interested in their own benefit than the greater good, least of all *your* benefit. Some people really *do* want to undermine others in some sort of twisted political popularity contest.

But **it doesn't matter.** This book is about **helpful philosophies**, and assuming that people are wanting to help you is one of the most helpful philosophies you can adopt.

And those people who you find to be insufferable, malicious, power-hungry vultures often turn around and surprise you when they encounter the unshakable optimism of someone who assumes the best of them (that'd be you). Difficult people can be your greatest allies, and *that's* a great political move—way better than looking good on some individual projects.

1. Put a "people want to help you" stickie where you'll see it regularly.

2. Ask for help, offer help.

3. Be grateful.

## DAY 20

# It doesn't really matter what people think

**M**ost of us spend our entire lives negotiating how other people feel about us, and how we feel about other people feeling the way they feel about us. It's a Russian nesting doll in a house of mirrors, to shake up a cocktail of metaphors. Seeking approval and avoiding rejection is such a central driving force that it's considered a psychological *handicap* if we *don't* (see: sociopaths).

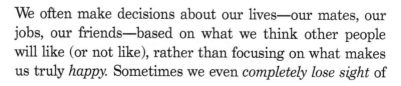 But in my experience, our insecurities have been sitting in the driver's seat of our lives for almost the entire road trip between Birth City and this little rest stop on the highway of life. And that's a problem. When we let our approval-seeking selves drive the car, we often end up in the swamp, being eaten by alligators. Usually metaphorically. *Hopefully* metaphorically.

We often make decisions about our lives—our mates, our jobs, our friends—based on what we think other people will like (or not like), rather than focusing on what makes us truly *happy*. Sometimes we even *completely lose sight* of what makes us happy in the interest of seeking the approval of people around us.

And then a funny thing happens (funny "oh no," not funny "haha"): the people around us only know the person who we think they'll like, not the actual person *who we are*. We take away their ability to like us for who we really are when we're so obsessed with being the person we think they want us to be.

When we stop caring what other people think and start pursuing our own happiness, we give other people something really solid about ourselves to get to know: We give them *us*.[2] **And we're pretty gosh darn spectacular.** (I mean, we've made it this far in life, so we've got to be pretty damn awesome.)

Freeing ourselves from obsessing about what others think of us is a path to a happier, more authentic life, with potential for connections on a much more genuine level.

But it's not so easy. It's not easy to just walk away from a lifetime (and, as I'll discuss shortly, a hereditary evolution) of self-consciousness.

## Back to the cavemen

There's a very good caveman reason for our instinct to seek approval from others. Back in the good ol' days, if someone thought we were "weird" or were otherwise put-off by our personality, appearance, manner of talking, or belief system, we could be ostracized, kicked out of the clan, and could never eat mastodon with our old hunting buddies again. It was *survival* back in those days, so our bodies developed a *visceral reaction* to rejection in order to protect us.

If you've ever been ashamed, embarrassed, mortified, or horrified, you've experienced your caveman brain at its best. And wasn't it awful? Didn't you suddenly and immediately want to conform as hard as you possibly could, as if your life depended on it?

Well, it kind of *did* depend on it. Once, a long time ago.

There was a great reason for this, too. Weirdos make noise during the hunt and foul up things for the whole clan (seriously, you squeak *one* clown nose during the hunt and all of a sudden you're "that asshole who ruins the hunt all the time"). Non-conformity was a problem for everyone, for survival-oriented reasons.

And evolution doesn't mess around, so it instilled in us a great need to be accepted and to shun people who we felt didn't conform.

## And then there's our parents...

Slightly more recently than about 200,000 years ago, when we were growing up, we were dependent on the approval of our parents. Our parents have the responsibility to prepare us for, and then thrust us into, the "real world" (which is only marginally less terrifying than a wilderness full of saber tooth tigers). They do this to the best of their ability by instilling in us the values that will make us productive members of society, able to find gainful employment, find a suitable mate, and raise similarly neurotic children (ok, maybe that was just me).

They pressure us to get good grades in the interest of getting a good job later. They pressure us to have good hygiene, wear flattering(ish) clothes (or at least pants most of the time), and talk to people with words that mostly make sense in order (hopefully). And if we don't conform to their standards, they threaten to kick us out and cut off our supply of mastodon meat (or whatever they had in your family).

Unfortunately, uniqueness doesn't tend to do well in classrooms (it looks a lot like "a problem child who might need some extra attention... might we suggest summer school?"). Being unique is a real liability, especially in families where parents don't have a lot of time to spare for their unique kid. "Trouble" is another word for "too unique to fit into our classroom tidily," so again, we're under a lot of pressure to conform.

## And then there's mothra-effing HIGH SCHOOL

Jesus Christ, don't even get me *started* on high school... well, ok, I kind of got myself started. I have no one but myself to blame. Per the usual.

High school is when most of us hit puberty and start asking ourselves the hard questions:

**1: What's that smell?**

**2: How can I get rid of this hair?**

Our bodies are squirting out adult hormones all over the place, and just like a three year-old with a catsup bottle, it's a bloody mess. In the worst case scenarios, I mean that *literally*.

At the same time our bodies are committing biological and social acceptability warfare against us, our peers are break-ing into factions of "cool" (i.e. "can eat mastodon with us") and "uncool" (i.e. "feed to saber tooth tigers"). Wearing the wrong thing on one day, or committing even a single social faux pas, or having an overly-oily and acne-prone face, can

send us spiralling into social rejection. If you're like me, that secret code of "right thing" must have been distributed in a class I never attended.

I remember one time in sixth grade, a girl in my class offhandedly mentioned that people think you're weird if you wear pants two days in a row. After that, I *never wore pants two days in a row*. To this day, I almost never wear pants. (I wear skirts or dresses... it's not like I'm wandering around without pants on. Usually.)

Because **one person in one class a hundred years ago told me it was weird.**

But even with my meticulous attention to the bit of fabric between my legs differentiating skirts and pants, I was terribly uncool in high school. I really did feel like I had missed out on the manual of acceptability, despite having purchased every *Seventeen* and *Glamour* magazine published between 1985 and 1993. *It didn't help that I was later diagnosed with mild Asperger Syndrome, which means that I miss most of the social cues that indicate acceptability.*

High school (and school in general) is when our need to be accepted—to be part of a tribe—is at its height, and for most of us, it's the time when we find our most profound rejections, either from our peers or members of the opposite sex.

It is a crucible of the formation of the importance of our social acceptability, and whether we conform or not can make the difference in what colleges we attend, what network we have as we enter the job market, and ultimately, our chances of success as we venture out into the world. No wonder it feels so high pressure!

The thing is, all that's *false.* Though our high school experience can help get us started, plenty of people who were losers in school go on to lead exciting, spectacular lives.

# Thank God we're beyond mastodons, right?!

Once we're out of the Stone Age, high school, and our parents' home, we really only need to seek approval from employers, friends, and potential romantic partners. But most of us are still stuck in a concern about what *the world at large* thinks about our acceptability.

Our concerns about our acceptability dictate everything from our style of dress to our choice of career. While our style of dress can lightly impact our happiness, our choice of career, mate, and friends can influence our whole quality of life. Making decisions about career, hobbies, partner, or social circle based on the opinions of others (be those family, friends, or random strangers we meet at networking events) can have *catastrophic* effects on our overall happiness.

The truth is, it doesn't matter what the vast majority of people think. What matters is that we are effective people with enough creativity to have a unique perspective. Bonus points if we have the vision and drive to execute plans based on our unique perspective.

## Overcoming the fear of rejection

We face a couple types of rejection, which are often confused in our brainmeats:

1. **Situational/conditional disapproval: when a person or people react(s) negatively to one thing we do (i.e. hearing the word "no," getting "the side-eye" from someone)**

**2. Complete rejection: when a person or people reject(s) us or dismiss(es) us entirely (i.e. stealing from a family member and being shunned by the whole family)**

While it can be completely devastating and potentially life threatening to get completely rejected (which is why so few of us steal from family members), it *isn't* life threatening to be given a hairy eyeball. But it *feels* life threatening.

But it *isn't*. It *really* isn't.

And it really doesn't matter what those people think. It won't kill you to get the hairy eyeball. It won't even kill you to be rejected by millions of people, as long as you find the people who will support and celebrate you, and you find an occupation that provides you enough money to live the life that brings you the most happiness.

( THE ARTIST ATTEMPTING TO DRAW A HAIRY EYEBALL )

When I feel mortified or seized by fear not to do something that I want to do, just because I feel like people will think I'm weird, I remember that their judgement of me is non-fatal. This has led to a lot of delightful experiences.

It's easier for me if I recall the separation between "embarrassed" and "isolating." When I'm embarrassed, that's an indication of a passing feeling: the non-fatal variety. When I'm feeling isolated, that's an indication that I'm feeling shame about who I am overall.

Embarrassment is survivable.

Isolation/shame is a much bigger deal for a different book. I recommend Brene Brown's book *Daring Greatly.*

## And people will be so delighted by you

A couple of years ago I ran into my friend Cameron in a parking lot. I saw him coming from a mile away, because he was wearing this *totally wild* Hawaiian shirt. In Los Angeles, only big-shot directors wear Hawaiian shirts, so his Hawaiian shirt stood out in the sea of black and silver cars like a shining beacon.

CAMERON IS AWESOME!

I couldn't stop smiling. His shirt made me so damn happy.

When he got closer, I loudly proclaimed his shirt *the absolute best shirt ever.*

And then he said something that changed how I see clothes, and ultimately completely changed the direction of my life: "Well, I figure if I can wear something that makes other people happy, I ought to!"

Which is how I ended up buying a bunch of pink fluffy princess dresses and gold shoes. It's also how I ended up with a rubber chicken purse filled with small rubber chickens that I'd hand out to anyone who asked about my purse.

Because that's seriously delightful.

Before The Cameron Revelation, I was a monochrome kind of gal. As a recovering goth, I used to wear almost entirely black or gray. It's easy to match, and mostly can be worn anywhere. But I realized it was also a **massive wasted opportunity to make people happy**.

We are walking opportunities to make people happy, and yet most of us are held back by the fear that some awful person we don't like anyways will give us the side-eye.

Now, lest you think I walk around in pink frilly princess dresses all the time, I must admit that I don't. Even I get tired of the toll that side-eye takes. Also, it's really hard to keep princess dresses ironed and wrinkle-free because OMG THOSE LAYERS OF RUFFLES. It's an endless ironing project.

But I do think my wardrobe is mostly made up of "remarkable" and semi-costume clothes—clothes that people see and say, "Hey! That's a great dress!" even though it takes more of a risk than I used to be comfortable taking.

I'm not *just* talking about clothing here, but clothing is one of the primary ways we open ourselves up to judgement from others, so it makes a great example. It could be your hair, your manner of speaking, your bold choice to show a bra strap in public, or your entire YOUNESS. Big and small, your uniqueness has a huge opportunity to delight people.

And if you're not gonna be you, who is?

Most people *love it* when they see other people expressing their individuality, which is why Cameron's shirt delighted me so much. It was HIM right out there in the open, being awesome, right all up in my face.

FABULOUS EXHIBIT A: YOU!

## "Judge not, lest ye be judged." - The Bible

Judging is kind of a chicken-and-egg situation: we feel judged by other people, so we judge other people. Except that instead of judging the people who judged us, we judge everyone else we meet from that point forward.

Someone has to end the cycle of judging, and it might as well be **you.**

We have to celebrate each other, and make each other feel good about our choices, positive about our bodies, and safe—really safe—being ourselves. The first step to doing that is to stop judging other people.

This means not talking shit about people or even *thinking* shit about people.

NO TALKING

Every person has gone through life with different trials and experiences, and we will never be able to understand where they're coming from, just like they can never truly understand where we're coming from. And that's ok. That's part of the beautiful diversity of life. It's amazing to me that we are able to communicate at all, and yet we manage to find ways to reach out to each other through our differences, and be friends, coworkers, partners, lovers.

It's a real miracle.

And part of honoring that miracle is accepting other people as they are, celebrating their perspective and experience, and appreciating them.

Try not to talk badly about other people, try not to complain about other people's behaviors, and try not to make judgements about other people overall. We're all just doing the best we can given the tools, information, and experience we have.

**ACTION STEP:** *Try something bold! Only you will know what is "bold" to you. Wear something fun, talk to a stranger, or go to the grocery store in your pajamas. It doesn't matter what people think—just be yourself without any concern.*

# Week 3 Review

This week we talked about possibly one of the most important functions of our lives as humans on this planet: our connections with other people. When we are good to each other—when we are good friends, specifically—and we have enough self-respect to insist that other people are good to us, we make people's lives better, and we make our own lives better.

Think about how an enthusiastic, supportive word from a good friend has turned around a day, and how you have the opportunity to pass that along to someone else. Think about the ripple effect you can create by being a positive person, and supporting other people's highest goals.

Our actions amplify exponentially, so the kindness you have sown this week will blossom flowers for the rest of people's lives.

Part 4:

THE TOOL KIT.

# The fastest goal-setting activity in the West

I am *bizarro bonkers insane* about the importance of making goals as part of a rich, full, and wonderful life. I would go so far as to say that without goals, meaningful existence is nigh impossible.

> *"Few people know so clearly what they want. Most people can't even think what to hope for when they throw a penny in a fountain."*
>
> **–BARBARA KINGSOLVER**

On the road of life, there are many tough times (I probably don't have to tell you that). Having clearly defined and written goals gives you something to work toward, and reminds you of what's important to you even on your hardest days.

On that super duper awful day, in the middle of a "SERIOUSLY? WHY DO I EVEN BOTHER?" episode, reviewing your goals can bring back calm, focus, and renewed energy to what might otherwise be a meaningless and frustrating slog.

The quicker you can get out of the slog and back on the road, the quicker you will achieve your goals.

Aside from giving our lives forward direction, they also can be powerful reminders of our past meaningful accomplishments. **Goals act as a checklist of things we have accomplished that are meaningful to us**.

You know of the stereotypical midlife crisis of "AAAH MY LIFE IS HALFWAY OVER AND WHAT HAVE I EVEN DONE?" followed by a careening and misguided hunt for any kind of meaning,  including such hits as "I quit my job to start a rock band," and "Look at my Ferrari Testarossa, bought on my credit card," and "I wanted to travel the world, but it never seemed to be the right time to leave work, and now my knees are all messed up so it's hard"?*

Well, those could have been well-executed, awesome goals. They could be things we look at and think "I did the heck out of that," rather than some panicked and poorly-executed grasping.

I care so deeply about goals that I made a video workshop that, as the proud owner of this book, you can get for free. After this book, go to danielleavincent.com/goalsworkshop to get a free goal workshop.

*This is my personal one, so please take this as a cautionary warning.

# What we're gonna do

We'll define a few of the goals that will get you started on achieving your dream life. Are these goals immutable and immovable? Of course not! Life is a fluid thing, and our priorities change. That's fine. Anything you work on here can and should be revisited and revised later.

A student of the goals course online said she had done her goals when she was in a pretty depressed place, so all her goals were kind of half-assed and depressed. So she went back and did the exercises again when she was in a better headspace, using her original goal list to measure against.

No matter what your present headspace, the important thing is to get started.

And you don't have to know how you're going to achieve these goals, either. I promise you, once you take the first few steps, the next steps will become apparent, and the next opportunities will open up for you.

I've said it before, and I'll say it again: **The path is made by walking**.

It's really important that you write these down (good thing you have your handy notebook!). That's as important as setting the goals themselves. It's not enough to just read through this and think "Yeah, I want a farm by 2020." You must write down these goals!

## Suzanne—California

I don't use the phrase "that changed my life" liberally. In fact I can only think of two other experiences that I can say that about. One is going thru a 10 day Vipassana sit and the other is having a child. And now the third is the goal writing workshop you offered.

The daydream section helped me get really clear on what I wanted my life to look like, and starting from something as simple as "what do I see when I wake up" was the perfect place to begin. All of a sudden I saw exactly what I wanted to do, and where I wanted to go with my business, life, and family. I also really appreciated that it covered all aspects of life. I did the goal writing workshop to gain focus and get tools to increase my income and jump start my business, but was reminded that life is all things; health & body, family, community, travel, downtime, personal goals as well as work goals.

Getting the to-do list whittled down to, 'ok, what do I have to do just today to move forward on my goals' - what it was 'just today' made everything seem attainable.

And taking a note from the Warren Buffett rule, I cut out the things that weren't getting me to my goals.

This is probably more than you asked for, but since I'm sharing, here are the changes I have made in my life since the goal workshop.

**Goal: Happy & Healthy home life with Buck and Milo**
Worked my way up to having my alarm go off at 5:45am. I now have an entire hour to myself, to read news, make my tea, collect my thoughts, wake up and not talk to anyone. I make Buck coffee every morning as a way to say I appreciate you. And an hour later when Buck and Milo wake up I'm awake, happy, and super stoked to see them, instead of frazzled, tired and not into talking to anyone.

**Goal: Gain strength back and drop body fat**
I generally make it to the gym at least 1-2x a week now, and even if I don't I try to do something that says "I am someone who exercises daily" even if it's just a push up, and I meditate every morning when I get to my office, before I start working, even if it's just for 2 minutes, and then say my goals out loud.

**Goal: Double my income**
I have added over 100 new potential clients to my mailing list by cold calling or emailing them to introduce myself and my company. I have gone to 5

industry mixers this year to network.  I have never done that before in my life!  And it fucking works.

**Goal:  Get my new show theatrics show fully funded**
I now have a 2 minute sizzle video, a complete creative pitch deck, and a 3 year P&L with ROIs for investors at 3 different investment levels and have 2 people shopping it.

Goals still to obtain are owning my dream home and owning an investment property, but the above goals will get me there.

Dude - I attribute all this awesomeness to doing that goal writing workshop!

## Throw "realistic" out the window

Don't worry about being realistic. The way your brain works, if you *want a thing*, you are physically capable of achieving it. Your brain can't conceive of things that are impossible, so it won't try to want them. If you want something, it is within your reach.

People struggle with this concept, but again, if we're going for "useful belief systems," you have to understand that this is very *useful.* Also, it turns out to be true in my observation.

Opportunities are there for you, if you look out for them. **The desire for the thing is proof that you can get it.**

You might be tempted to write down only goals that you think you can achieve—to "be reasonable." I'm going to let you in on a little secret: if you achieve all the goals you have written down, you have REALLY underestimated your goals. These goals should be *life fulfilling,* and a fulfilling life is often a little of a stretch.

Accept that you might not achieve all these goals—heck, if you do achieve all of them, 1. HOLY MOLY, LOOK AT YOU AND YOUR GOAL ACHIEVEMENT! And 2. Please set more ambitious goals, because you are clearly underestimating how amazing you are.

## But what if I fail?

The only reason that people don't go for the goals of their biggest and wildest ambitions is because the goals closest to our hearts hurt the most when we don't achieve them. There's nothing quite as heartbreaking as truly going for something with all our hearts, minds, souls, and bodies, and then just plain old not getting it.

I want to look at that up close and personal, because we'd be sweeping an elephant under the rug if we didn't look at it.

Sometimes we're really gonna go for it, and we're just not going to get it. We might do everything in our power to make things come together, but for whatever reason, things just don't happen.

First, go back and check out Day 12, "When things go wrong, they have actually gone right." There may be some greater purpose in the immediate "failure" that will turn out to be a huge win in the future.

But even if you go for a goal and fail to achieve it, you will—I guarantee—achieve a higher goal. You'll be a better person. You'll be closer to achieving that goal in the future, and you'll be clearer about the circumstances you need to create in order to achieve that goal.

So don't worry about failure. You'll survive. Humans are durable creatures, and you've already proven that you're a survivor.

ACTION STEP:

*In your notebook, write down a day in your dream life. It doesn't have to be all of your dream life, just one part of it. If you're inspired, go ahead and really go for it, but if that seems daunting, then just do one day.*

## My Action Steps...

My perfect day starts with waking up on a California King size bed with really great sheets.

I hear the ocean and the breeze is blowing through the screened windows. I can smell the salty air and see the outline of the curtains. The sun isn't anywhere near up yet, and dawn is just sneaking around the horizon quietly, but I smell the coffee brewing from the other room and it seems a good time to get up.

I have a cup of coffee on the porch, and a fruit salad with fresh local fruit. Leaving the dishes on the porch, I walk down to the water and it's warm and inviting. I wade out and stand there, feeling the water line on my stomach, which is fit and toned from regular exercise. I close my eyes and the morning's words start coming into my head, so I turn and swim back to shore in an attempt to catch them before they scamper off.

I start cooking breakfast and write some of the words in my notebook just to remember them, and then I take my breakfast out to the porch with my laptop and write for an hour.

Ready to take a break, I go fix Russ some breakfast and bring it to him in bed, laying down and drinking coffee in bed with him as he wakes up. Our ridiculous dogs, which had been previously sound asleep, are now running all over the place trying to attract his attention for bacon scraps.

After breakfast, I go back to writing for a couple more hours. Words come easily, and are more vivid and colorful than when I'm working from my regular home in Grass Valley. Grass Valley is good for planning and editing. Hawaii is good for writing.

By noon, I am ready for another break. I fix some lunch—some fruit and salad and leftover fish—and eat it on the porch looking out on the beach. More words, which I write down in my notebook.

I am not ready to go back to writing yet, and go fill my bath in the bathroom with the french doors opening onto the front porch. I sit in the bath, pondering what productivity means, and how I might achieve that while also achieving... this moment, which is perfect. It's cool enough that there's a breeze through the doors, and the warm bath is just wonderful. I lay back and clear my mind.

After the bath, I put on my afternoon sundress and go back to writing. Yes, there's a lot of writing. But this is why I'm here. By 2pm, I will be all worded out, so I have to get the writing in while it lasts.

And 2pm rolls around, so I close my laptop and finish work for the day. I find Russ reading on the back balcony in his hammock... or, rather, he's sleeping under a book that he was reading. I wake him up and we go downstairs, grab our kayaks, and wade into the water. We kayak out to the mouth of the bay where the waves get a little exciting, and the sea spray is fresh and cool.

We kayak back to the house, taking the long way, and seeing the fish through the clear, still water.

Russ fixes an early dinner and we watch the sunset from the front porch, chatting and laughing while the clouds finish their showy dance in the sky.

All of life is wonderful. My heart and mind are at peace, and I feel my mind opening to receive the

world's information in the night so I can wake up
and start writing again the next morning.

Day 23:
# CONTEXT
## of YOUR
# PERFECT DAY

This is an *outstandingly abbreviated* version of my entire goal-setting process, so I'd really love for you to get the full goal-setting experience by taking my free online goal-setting workshop here: *danielleavincent.com/goalsworkshop*

U nless you just basically wrote a journal entry of your current life, you probably have to change, grow, and adjust in order to wake up in your dream life.

We need to figure out what all's happening in this perfect day. We need to flesh it out so we can get a clearer picture of what it looks like.

If you're not sure about the details around your perfect day, again I repeat to you: that's ok. It's fine to guess, and it's also fine to have many answers. For example, my perfect day is getting up at dawn in a tropical paradise. But that doesn't mean that my entire life is the same every single day, because my actual perfect life would include a variety of experiences and locations. One day might be coffee on the patio and a nice drive to my factory, but a week from that day might be sitting under a waterfall in Hawaii, and a month from that might be sitting in a cafe in Barcelona.

Today's the day where you color in some of the details around that isolated day.

ACTION STEPS:

*1. Go back to the exercise where you wrote out your perfect day.*

*2. Put yourself in the mindset of you, however far in the future that day is. Look around in your imagination and take inventory of the below characteristics of what that future you is like.*

This should be a fun and refreshing exercise. I mean, it's your perfect life! Really let your imagination go wild here!

## ATTITUDE

*Write down the attitude of the you in that perfect day. Are you confident in your abilities? Do you feel in control of things around you? Are you carefree or are you meticulously working on things? What are you feeling on that day?*

### My Action Steps...

I am confident and diligent. I am clear about what
I'm writing, and the words are easy. I also am not
worried at all. I am focused, but calm..

## PEOPLE

*Who is around you? Who is in your life? Who are the people helping you and supporting you? Who are the people you are helping and supporting? Do you have family? A life partner? Many partners?*

Russ is here. My family is around and healthy. I
know I have friends and people back home. I'd want
a life where I could visit those friends and go on
road trips to see them and meet them where they are.
I also know that our business is taken care of by
competent people, so I don't have to worry about
what's happening back home when we're away.

## CAREER

*What are you doing for a living? Are you in a higher position? Is your job one that can be done from anywhere? From the corner office? Are you retired? Are you freelancing? Are you full-time? Do you have your own business?*

I write, but I also have Outlaw Soaps, which is doing well. I have a diverse job set, but most of my tasks can fit into a few hours per day.

## LOCATION

*Where are you? What is around you? Is this your home? An office? Your own building? The beach? A mountain?*

In a tropical paradise, tbd. I envision having a place where we go to vacation and to write, but also a home base in Grass Valley.

## HEALTH

*What is your health like? Are you agile? Strong? Flexible? How do you feel?*

I am toned and healthy and strong. All tasks are easy to me because I am in great physical shape. I am at a comfortable weight that allows for easy movement and I'm comfortable in my clothes.

# GETTING THERE FROM HERE

## OK! Now we're cookin' with gas (in a safe space with plenty of ventilation)!

**N**ow that you've written down the context of your dream life, you can start thinking about the steps that it would take to get there.

Brian Tracy, the master of all goal-setting, points out in his book *Goals!: How to Get Everything You Want—Faster Than You Ever Thought Possible*, that in order to achieve what you want to achieve, you're going to have to become the person who can achieve those goals. If you were already the person who could have that perfect day-in-the-life, you'd already be there in that perfect day.

But you're not, so today, we're going to figure out some first steps to get there from here.

*For each of the characteristics you wrote about yesterday, write one thing that could put you on the path to having that characteristic. For example, if you want to start your own business and you don't know what kind of business you want to start, you might want to write down* **"brainstorm potential business ideas."** *If you want to get a promotion, think about what kind of education or career moves you'd have to make in order to get that promotion. You might even start with* **"ask boss what it would take to get a promotion."**

Hey! Look at that! You've got a rough map of how to get from here to your dream life! Pretty snazzy!

**My Action Steps...**

## ATTITUDE

(I am confident and diligent. I am clear about what I'm writing, and the words are easy. I also am not worried at all. I am focused, but calm.)

· · · Practice. I need to practice writing, I need to practice making time for my writing, and I need to practice exercising mindfulness so I am not stressed out even when I have a lot of stuff going on.

## PEOPLE

(Russ is here. My family is around and healthy. I know I have friends and people back home. I'd want a life where I could visit those friends and go on road trips to see them and meet them where they are. I also know that our business is taken care of by competent people, so I don't have to worry about what's happening back home when we're away.)

· · · I need to make more time to connect in person with the people who are important to me. We need to go see them.

## CAREER

(I write, but I also have Outlaw Soaps, which is doing well. I have a diverse job set, but most of my tasks can fit into a few hours per day.)

· · · I need to work on my book (huzzah!), and also make sure Outlaw Soaps is in a place that can be managed remotely.

## LOCATION

(In a tropical paradise, tbd. I envision having a place where we go to vacation and to write, but also a home base in Grass Valley for while we're at the workshop. It's a good space for relaxing and planning.)

· · · I think we're planning a trip to Hawaii in late March, and we will scout perfect locations while we are there..

## HEALTH

(I am toned and healthy and strong. All tasks are easy to me because I am in great physical shape. I am at a comfortable weight that allows for easy movement and I'm comfortable in my clothes.)

· · · I am already in the process of achieving this. I work out three times per week and am at a comfortable weight.

# How to keep a journal

By now, you've (hopefully?) been writing in your notebook for a few weeks, so writing in a notebook daily should feel pretty solid for you.

T he tricky part about keeping a journal is that:

**1. It's hard for it not to become a bottomless bitchfest**

**2. All that unstructured space is sometimes daunting**

Journals are beneficial because they enable you to see patterns in your life, they help you work out solutions to complex problems, and they act as a great reminder of territory you've already covered.

When I was quitting drinking, it was really helpful for me to go back over my journals and read that in fact, about one out of four days I commented about how hungover I was. That was unacceptable, since it meant that I had essentially not performed my best on that day. And that doesn't even include the days I was mildly hungover but didn't think to mention it in my journal! YIPE.

I have used my journal to track things like how medication is affecting me, what my PMS cycle is doing to my moods and general life outlook, and even mundane stuff like business planning and expectations.

I use my journal to unload about my goals. A couple weeks before we found our dream home, I outlined in very minute detail all the qualities that I wanted our new home to have. When Russ went to check out this house (the one I'm writing this in), it was easy to identify that we should rent this very one, since I had described it in unreal detail. **This was the house I wrote about.**

I talked about the power of writing in the goals workshop, but don't think that writing-stuff-into-reality is just confined to the goals workshop. Oh no! You can summon that awesomeness any time at all! Just break out your journal and get to writing!

There are no rules about how to use a journal, just as long as you use it with enough regularity that you don't feel burdened by "starting up again." For me, daily is that cadence. If I miss a day, it's not such a big deal. But if I miss two days, I start feeling behind, and like I need to "catch up." Too much happens, I have too many thoughts, and it gets harder and harder to open the journal and just dash off a quick entry.

There are several ways of keeping a journal, so if you've tried to journal in the past and haven't found it useful, read on.

## The morning pages

Popularized in *The Artist's Way* (a great book, by the way), the Morning Pages is an exercise where you write three pages of *whatever* every morning. It's a brain dump of all the unprocessed noise rumbling around in your brain like gravel in your mouth.

It's straightforward: three pages, content is irrelevant, unfailingly every morning.

## What worked, what didn't

This one is from my friend Beth. She keeps a daily journal of the things that worked and the things that didn't work. Yep, that simple. I'm sure you can see how this would also be tremendously helpful.

## Freeform journaling

This is my method. I carry my journal with me *everywhere* and I work out darn near *everything* in the journal. As soon as this chapter's over, I'm probably going to write about how I'm writing this book, and that it's really hard, and then I'll brainstorm ways to break down the task into smaller tasks (yes, smaller than 30 days), and then hopefully I'll come up with some good solutions.

I write about events that happened, and hopes I have for the future. I write about goals that I have, and I even work out budgets if I need some private scribble-space.

I keep all my journals because I find it helpful to go back and read past journals.

## For finding your direction

My friend Janet and I were talking about the importance of journaling the other day. She is a coach and friend to many people at many points in their lives, and recommends they start journaling as the first course of action when people come to her for direction.

She has a three-question guided journaling practice, which takes exactly a half hour every morning. Answer each question for 10 minutes (just set a timer), no more, no less. Even if you have nothing to say, just ramble with whatever comes into your head. That's the nature of journaling sometimes: you just keep rambling, and eventually some order comes around. Or no order comes around, and order comes around some other day. It's all fine.

Her three questions are:

1. **What do I love doing?**

2. **What gives me energy?**

3. **What unique skills, experiences, and perspectives do I have that nobody else has?**

For each of these questions, just answer them every day, the same questions, for 10 minutes each. Over time, you will gain clarity about your interests and direction!

. . . . . . . . . . . . . . . . . . . . . . . . . . . . . . . . . . . . . . . . . . . . . . . . . . . . . . . . . . . . . . . . . . . . . . . . . . . . . . . . . . . . . . . .

*Today's action step is to... surprise! Write in your journal. Just for a little while, for a few pages, about what you're thinking, how you're feeling, and maybe even about this process of starting a journal!*

# MEDITATION

Joining forces with the Universe because you're one with the Universe.

Meditation is just the practice of being mentally and physically still for some amount of time.

I
t sounds easy, right? Just clear your mind and sit with your eyes closed for 20 minutes.

But it's not quite so easy. It's hard to quiet your mind enough to focus on one thing—your breath, for example—before thoughts start hustling their way in, demanding to be heard and addressed. And then we (or at least I) feel like I'm "bad at meditation" and then my brain comes up with all the reasons why I really don't have time to meditate and probably don't need to meditate anyways.

> *"Reality is merely an illusion, albeit a very persistent one."*
>
> **—ALBERT EINSTEIN**

## Why meditate?

Throughout all of history, the most enlightened spiritual leaders have insisted that *everything is* **one**, and our individuality is just illusion. But that illusion is a *super duper persistent illusion*, so we get caught up in the illusion, totally forgetting that the reality is that **we're all one** with everything—the trees, the ground, the rocks, the birds, the grass, and even other people.

When we're going along in our regular lives, our individuality blocks the reality of this one-ness. We have individual-person problems like having to pay another individual person rent, going to work and dealing with another individual person's anger management issues, and even sitting in traffic with what feels like 8 million other individuals, all trying to get to apparently the same place we're going.

Meditation is the portal we have into The One-ness.

When we meditate, we are able to connect to the one life-force in The Universe. If that didn't give you a little shudder, you aren't quite realizing the awesomeness of it... **you** are part of The Universe, and that includes everything of everything.

So when you connect to The Universe, your wishes, dreams, and desires enter into The Universe straight away, just like rain on the ocean.

And yes, there are other ways of conveying your wishes to The Universe (prayer is a popular one), but meditation is the most straightforward and pan-denominational.

Not only that, the directions that come to you when you're meditating are straight from The Universe, too. The same Universe that is working for everyone's best interest. When you meditate, you can get direction and insight on situations, problems, and your life, that will bring the greatest good to the greatest number of people.

I'm not dicking around with unproven technology here, this is the real deal: Universal Truth.

# The rational voice

My friend Ray (see story on p. 218) and I were talking about the shift in perspective that comes with regular meditation. It's difficult to sense and even more difficult to describe, but in our best attempt, we called it "the rational voice."

Most of us go through our lives reacting. We are like a float of ping-pong balls on a rushing river, bouncing between waves, springing off rocks, and being tossed in unpredictable directions.

Over time, meditation seems to give us a thoughtful, reflective, rational voice that responds first, interjecting between the action and the reaction, saying, "Wait, let's think about this. What is the truly best course of action here?" Whether we're responding to someone's unpleasant tone, news of an accidental charge on our bank account, or any other unexpected and frustrating event, the rational voice gives us an opportunity to reflect. It gives us options rather than forcing us to just *act.*

Of all the gifts of meditation, the rational voice has been the most useful to me personally. It gives me perspective and control.

# Health

As if communicating directly with The Universe and being equipped with a first-responder rational voice wasn't enough, meditation has been scientifically proven to have significant health benefits.

Studies have shown marked improvement for symptoms ranging from lower back pain to insomnia.[3] One study even suggested that meditation could increase empathy and decrease suicidal thoughts (it's probably that "rational voice" I was just talking about).

According to Richard J. Davidson, Ph.D at the University of Wisconsin-Madison[4], meditation has the power to literally transform your brain, even changing lifelong mental conditions like anxiety disorders, and even autism. Davidson says that meditation trains your brain, bringing it under better control, which has profound effects.

In addition to training your brain, meditation can even lower your blood pressure[5] and may be an effective treatment to reduce hot flashes for women in menopause.[6]

Meditation is powerful stuff and it's totally free. Given all these benefits, don't you think it's worth incorporating into your daily life?

[3] Source: nccih.nih.gov/health/223/research
[4] Source: nccih.nih.gov/news/events/lectures/SES16
[5] Source: news.bbc.co.uk/2/hi/health/410003.stm
212   [6] Source: nccih.nih.gov/health/providers/digest/menopause-science#heading4

# How to meditate

For a practice that basically includes sitting still and thinking of nothing, there are a lot of opinions on the best ways to meditate. Oprah Winfrey even bought all of us at her company Transcendental Meditation courses, which are *quite expensive*. But in all my methods and years of meditation, I haven't found any to be consistently superior to any other, so I'll share the basics:

Get in a quiet place.

Sit in a comfortable position. You could sit with both feet on the floor, or in the cross-legged position, but try not to be all curled up on yourself. Expand into the space around you, don't collapse.

Put your phone in airplane mode.

Set a timer for 20 minutes.

Close your eyes.

Clear your mind.

When the alarm goes off, you're done meditating. Rest a few seconds until you "come back" to yourself, and go on about your day.

# Clearing your mind

Ok, I put it there in the bullets just like it was a one-and-done kind of deal, but that's the trickiest and most uncomfortable part of the whole thing. I have been meditating pretty regularly for *years*, and I still can't consistently clear my mind.

Here are some techniques I use to keep my mind clear as things come up:

1. **Acknowledge the thought and say to myself "it can wait for 20 minutes.** I can set it aside for just 20 minutes" and then visualize it floating away until it's a little vanishing speck on the horizon.

2. **Envision a pond with ripples that gradually settle down into a glassy pool.**

3. **Count my breath as one, two, three, four seconds in, holding for one second, and then one, two, three, four, five seconds out, holding for one second, repeat.**

4. **Repeat a mantra such as "for the greatest good" or "all is one."**

For Pete's sake, don't beat yourself up for having thoughts come into your head. This doesn't make you "bad at meditating" or mean it "isn't working." It means you're a human being. **Everyone** has thoughts.

Buddhists call this "Monkey Mind," for reasons that probably are obvious if you've tried meditating. Your mind is all over the place like a monkey on methamphetamines, flinging poo and trying anything to get your attention, and it's REALLY DANG ANNOYING when you're just trying to have a pleasant sit-down with The Universe.

But trust me, you get better. *It* gets better. As you practice, you might not get perfect, but at least you'll get better and more quiet.

## Why 20 minutes?

Sitting still for 20 minutes is a real commitment. I'm not gonna lie: I don't do it every day. It's embarrassingly difficult to take 20 sequential minutes of silence. I always feel like I absolutely *should* be able to take 20 minutes with consistency, considering how good it is. And then life gets in the way, with one thing, and then another thing, and pretty soon it's the end of the day, and I'm exhausted.

Because of this, I try to take my 20 minutes before my day gets started, before anyone else is awake. I have a cup of coffee, just so I don't fall asleep, and then I sit on the couch, both feet squarely on the floor, and I set my meditation timer. Sometimes, thoughts come to me during meditation and, unless they seem to be a God-given insight, I softly set them aside.

But it's important to take 20 minutes if you can, and here's why: something happens. The nature of meditation shifts from being a brief interval (say, for example, 5 minutes) to achieving a stillness. It's like riding a rodeo bull: under 15 minutes is amateur, but the real prize is for those who stay in the saddle for the full 20.

At around minute 10, my monkey mind starts wondering what time it is. By minute 12 or 13, I start fantasizing that maybe my timer broke or crashed, and maybe I should just look at the clock. Since I've been doing this for a few years,

I know the bizarrely repetitive and predictable thought pattern, so I remind myself that this is "minute 12 anxiety," and remind myself to settle down, that it's only for 20 minutes, and that my monkey is just rattling the cage.

Twenty minutes is enough time to unlock profound meditation experiences that, with practice, can really blow your mind.

I have been one with a bumble bee seeking out dogwood blossoms, feeling the tickle of the petals and the wind from the beating of my wings. I have been that dogwood blossom, celebrating the bee's arrival and rolling out the petal carpet for him. I have been one with the air—with *all* the air—around the planet. I have been the ocean, swelling and bulging with the tides, attracted to my friend the moon.

I have also thought of nothing but the content for this week's email newsletter, lost in my thoughts, until the timer goes off and I am disappointed in myself for letting that opportunity for stillness slip by.

I have also gone into meditation with a problem, set my intention to have the answer revealed to me, cleared my mind, and had the solution come to me like a butterfly. For those times, I do break meditation long enough to write down the revelation, and then return to meditating with deep gratitude.

Meditation gets easier the more you practice it, but even masters struggle with the same things beginners do. It's hard to find the time, and even when we find it, it's hard to truly be still. 20 minutes give us that time.

# Meditation tools

It will probably surprise you not-at-all that there's an app for that.

Yep, there are *bazillions* of meditation apps, including guided meditations and everything.

### THE CHOPRA CENTER

The Chopra Center (of that guy Deepak who knows all the cool and enlightened stuff) has regular free "21 Day Meditation Experiences" (they used to call them "Meditation Challenges," but I think the idea of a challenge was a little too non-meditational). The Chopra Meditation Experiences open with some meditative thoughts (depending on the theme of the experience), give you a handy Sanskrit mantra to repeat, give you some minutes of music, and then close.

They're absolutely *stellar* for beginners, because you get stuff to think about, you get a mantra, and you get someone timing the experience for you. You also get a daily sequence, so it encourages daily participation.

### INSIGHT MEDITATION TIMER

This app has it all. The primary function of the app is a meditation timer, but it also includes guided meditation (including some to aid with sleep). There's even a very fine community where you can thank other people for meditating with you (you know, since they joined in with The Universe at the same time 'n' all).

## OTHER FORMS OF MEDITATION

"Exercise is my meditation."

"I find walking through the forest to be a good meditation."

"When I'm on my motorcycle, it quiets and focuses me. It is my meditation."

While I appreciate that people are trying to work meditation into other soothing and relaxing activities, *meditation isn't just any relaxing activity.* Meditation is sitting still and clearing your mind.

There is no substitute for literally meditating.

If you find meditation to be too difficult, I understand that. But don't use how difficult meditation is to justify pivoting on the concept of meditation to the more general, umbrella concept of relaxing.

Meditation isn't relaxing. It is sometimes *work.* It requires diligence. It is a mindful practice that is not necessarily easy.

But it's *important.*

---

## A Story from Ray—California

I began my journey with meditation six years ago.
The company I work for offered free training and I

thought, "Why would I do that?" I didn't think I "needed" it. Then someone reminded me, "It's free, why not?" That was a good point, so I signed up.

Soon after, I went to a training session and was walked through the process. No epiphany occurred, but it was relaxing. My job seemed to require me getting interrupted every 5 minutes, and 20 minutes of quiet was a welcome reward for meditating.

After a few weeks, a conversation among some office friends turned to meditation and how much they liked it. Someone said, "Yeah, it really helped me, but nothing like what it has done for you."

The "you" in that sentence was me.

As unexpected "compliments" can do, that sentence embedded into my brain like a serrated thumbtack. Was it sincere? A backhanded compliment? A joke at my expense? I cycled through emotions from being embarrassed, to angry that I was embarrassed, and then embarrassed for being angry, all the while trying to convince myself I was blowing it out of proportion. That's when I realized how reactive, stressed, and quick-tempered I was.

Oddly I noticed this self-evaluation from an external perspective, which I never did before. The benefit of which was having this honest conversation with myself without feeling too awkward about it.

That was the epiphany. They were right, meditation did help me.

I did feel embarrassed for a moment but realized it didn't matter. The world really isn't all about me. I can't explain the steps meditating allowed me to take to get to that point—that can probably be explained in the science of it all, I'd guess—but I know realizing it made life so much easier and more enjoyable.

That epiphany lasted a few seconds. I smiled for a moment and remembered something I said to a friend once, "You're way too amazing of a person to waste your time being angry." It was a bit ironic how I had the answer to the question I didn't know I was asking all along. Meditating just helped me to see it.

...................................................................................

**ACTION STEP:**

*I want you to try meditating as I have outlined it here for at least 10 minutes every day. If you can work up to 20 minutes, great. If you can work up to 20 minutes, twice per day, awesome.*

# CAREER COUNSELING

T his is a subject for an entirely different book, but since it forms so much of our lives, this book wouldn't be complete without a look at our career, or as I like to call it, our "series of loosely related pursuits that people give us money for."

I would describe my "career" as the experience of a puppy running through a field, finding something interesting and rolling in it, and then dashing off in search of a new and potentially more exciting smell. I have been very lucky—one might even call it "blessed"—with an incredibly lucrative and diverse career path.

I blame the Victorian novel *Sister Carrie* for my attitude toward work.

*Sister Carrie* is a cautionary tale about a young lady (Carrie, of course) who moves from a rural town into the big, fancy city of Chicago. When she moves there, she immediately starts working for a shoe factory, which is discouragingly rough and brutish. She becomes involved with a rich sales-man (Drouet), who is taken in by her "unspoilt beauty." He buys her a bunch of clothes, sets her up in an apartment, and through a bunch of ups and downs, and various relationships, she generally falls from grace in the most spectacular Victorian fashion. Older men deteriorate in her presence, trying to get her favors and attention. Meanwhile, she uses her network to get acting gigs, which she has always been interested in pursuing, and Carrie ultimately leaves a wake of wrecked men behind her as she charms and then abandons each, in turn. One of them even commits suicide in a homeless shelter after embezzling money and leaving his wife and kids. I mean, horror.

Ultimately, Carrie achieves stardom and fame, but finds that money, baubles, and furs no longer thrill her like they used to, and she wishes for simpler times.

You may wonder why I found so much inspiration from this story.

No, it's not because I aspire to be an actress, or to step on men on my way up the ladder. It's because at its core, *Sister Carrie* is about being adaptable, about seeing opportunities in the ether, about grabbing them, and about always being open to trying new things. I see Carrie as the unlikely hero of the story, showing an agility of perspective that none of the other characters have, which ultimately leads her to success, and them to ruin.

Carrie also isn't afraid to pursue what she wants, and to do things to "make it work" (as Tim Gunn says), even if those things are distasteful to the sensibilities of the day. Back in

Victorian times, those distasteful things included premarital sex with older men. Hey, she did what she wanted to do. But in these modern times, premarital sex with older men probably won't raise as many eyebrows as, say, quitting a desk job to start a consulting business, or opening an indie coffee shop a block away from Starbucks.

Carrie didn't have any problems dropping what wasn't working for her. When she worked in the shoe factory, she just went in and decided, "Welp, this sure as heck isn't for me." So she found something else. She was never stuck. She never wrung her hands about how much of a bummer it was that she was stuck in the factory job, but that she needed to keep the job for 10 years until she could work up enough money to move out on her own.

She was never the victim of her circumstances—if anything, her circumstances were the victim of *her*.

And finally, our hero comes to realize that the money isn't really what it was about after all. She seems to really love acting, and worked her way up from some bit parts as a chorus girl, to a starring role.

Carrie went for it. And yeah, back in the Victorian times, this was a tragic tale of a young woman corrupted by the big city. But to me, this is the story of a life well-lived. She had adventures, she laughed, she got what she wanted, and she learned what she didn't want... all this was immeasurably better than staying planted on a rural farm in Wisconsin and spending her life wishing she could experience a life of adventure.

# Work to live or live to work? Please, let's not have this conversation

You may have heard the old maxim, "Are you living to work, or working to live?" The former, apparently, meaning you lack work-life balance, the latter meaning your work is supporting your "real life."

I think this is the wrong way of looking at work *and* life.

Work is part of life, and life is part of work. It must be an integrated whole, which includes all your other pursuits and interests, like family, friends, recreation, and personal fulfillment. I think work is one of the core elements of personal fulfillment.

There are a lot of reasons people get tied up in the whole "live to work" thing, and mostly those have to do with feelings of fear, duty, and responsibility. We get trapped in a rut-based worldview, where the things we enjoy and find personally fulfilling seem out of reach, or like a part of our job that has gone away, but we feel like we "need" this job anyways.

We succumb to the feelings that we must "be realistic." We would rather hide our light under a bushel than look for the opportunities and take the risks associated with pursuing our ambitions for an exciting career/life.

## The world doesn't penalize unicorns anymore

Every traditional social construct that rewards conformity and penalizes uniqueness (high school, for example) is from a different time, with different survival criteria.

All that paranoia, anxiety, and worry is *completely useless*. It doesn't make us more suitable mates, friends, or employees, it makes us dispensable. Replaceable. Boring.

As our culture moves away from factory work, the people who are best able to survive are the creative and unique people—the *unicorns*. Robots and large-scale manufacturing plants in other countries are taking on the jobs that require conformity. The *interesting* and *amazing* jobs all require exceptional people with exceptional vision.

*Conforming and making decisions based on what we think other people will approve of is no longer a survival skill, it is a liability.*

Don't you want an *interesting* and *amazing* job? HECK YES you do!

Think of the most successful people of our culture today: Oprah? Steve Jobs (RIP)? Bill Gates? Heck, even The Rock?

Do any of those people care about conforming? Oh, probably they struggle with it (or did before they overcame it), but their uniqueness is what they *based their fame on.*

And people love them *and hate them.* They are certainly not everyone's cup of tea. If we were in a caveman society, they would all be saber tooth cat food (ok, except maybe The Rock, because he'd look so good in saber tooth skin that a saber tooth would likely volunteer his coat). They'd be terrible for the hunt because they act in unpredictable ways. They don't conform.

But even beyond celebrities, every major social, technological, or economic breakthrough has been done by people who had a ton of haters. Not just "not my cup of tea"-ers, but HATERS.

Now, I'm not suggesting that you run out and get a bunch of haters by, say, burning an effigy of your local president. Just having haters alone isn't enough to propel you into lasting, positive societal contribution and wealth, but developing a healthy disregard for the vast majority of people's opinions is a great start to a life of fulfillment.

## I draw tremendous strength from Lady Gaga

However you feel about her music, you gotta hand it to Lady Gaga: she really has made the world a safer place to be freaky.

When we're thinking about the **big deal risks**, like decisions to quit our job at the hospital and become a musician, I find it helpful to find a patron saint.

For whatever enterprise you're undertaking, there's an entire *world* full of people who have done it before you, and many of them have pulled it off with great panache and success.

And if they can do it, my friend, so can you.*

Whether you want to wear a questionably appropriate outfit to a party (is it really a *pink frilly princess dress* kind of event?) or quit your job to launch a high-end cosmetic brush company (yes, it has been done! I met someone who did just that!), there are bold pioneers who have gone before you and done it... and you can find them, read about them, and maybe even talk to them!

They have crossed the bridge of unacceptability in their process, and you can find courage in their courage.

The internet is an amazing thing. It connects people and enables them to share experiences on a level never before possible.

We can literally see what Oprah had for dinner.

Find a "patron saint" (really, just anyone whose accomplishments you admire) and read about the steps they took to accomplish what you are hoping to accomplish. Along the way, they faced some heavy rejection, hurdles (both personal and external), and definitely more than a little stink-eye. Imagine what kind of internal fortitude it took to overcome those fears and worries and imagine yourself full of that fortitude.

If they can do it, you can do it.

If you want to find more unlikely success stories where people faced tremendous social pressure *not* to accomplish

---

*This was a revelation to me. I was listening to some lectures from Jim Rohn and he said that you could achieve the same results as someone else, just by doing what they do. He said that, sure, luck and skill sometimes play a factor, but just showing up and doing the thing is the single biggest predictor of success.

what they later accomplished, just Google "unlikely success stories" and sit in awe and admiration of these brave souls.

As a small business owner, I can assure you that the most difficult part of having a small business is not the money, the employees, the sales, or the product. The most difficult part is having the tenacity to go forward, *even though many people reject our products, and sometimes me, personally.* I just have to keep going forward.

And you have that tenacity. That tenacity is nothing more than just moving forward even when you don't feel like moving forward, and you have it.

## But what about money?

In order to survive in this society, we have to have money. But there are as many ways to make money as there are people in this world, so if you think that you have to stay in a job "because you need the money," you're wasting your life. There are millions of people making a living doing things they love, and plenty of them have less education or family wealth than you do.

You are as entitled to a job you love just as much as anyone. If they can have it, you can have it.

This is not to say you should just quit your job tomorrow and let The Universe catch your back (hey, it might work, but I'm not going to be the one to advise you on that course), but it's really worth it to your *whole life* to engineer a money-making strategy that works for what you want to do in your lifetime. Most of us spend *a lot of time* doing things in order to make money, so it's really in our best interest to figure out exactly how much money we need, and what we want to do to make it.

My friend and her husband recently got back from Kauai, Hawaii, and had such a profound experience that they decided to re-evaluate their entire lives to see if they could arrange a several-month-long trip there.

*Anything is possible,* you just have to take a step back and figure out how to make the puzzle fit together.

## The job that you "need"

When my friend Beth graduated with her Doctorate of Applied Statistics, she knew she had to find a job *right away.* Her student loans were looming ominously on the near horizon and she didn't have a ton of financial runway to get off the ground. So, she hit the bricks. She started applying for the statistical analyst jobs that were at her level, both in the for-profit and nonprofit sectors, and going for interviews.

She's a spectacularly brilliant person, so she had a lot of interested companies courting her, but she'd go into the interviews, look around, and feel revulsion at the cube life. All of them were in-cubicle jobs. The work itself seemed fine, but going to an office and sitting in a cubicle, surrounded by other coworkers chatting and generally being distracting, sounded like a Hellscape.

"When I was describing the work environment to my therapist, I started crying. I knew I couldn't work there."

The situation was getting critical. She was afraid she'd just have to take one of these jobs. She was getting offers, and they wanted to know what she wanted to do.

But it just wasn't what she wanted! She wanted a more flexible work environment! Maybe even part-time, where she could work from home, or wherever she happened to be. She wanted to work with people who were passionate about their jobs, working on interesting and meaningful projects.

But as the months dragged on, it looked like maybe that was just a unicorn.

She held out with tooth-gritting determination and then— PHEW—she got a job that is *exactly* what she was looking for, with a terrific and flexible boss, working from home, doing projects she finds truly engaging and interesting.

She found the unicorn.

And she loves it. She just took a week and a half off to go to Burning Man, which her work was totally cool with. She gets to be her unique and amazing self *and* a brilliant statistician.

## You have to know the unicorn

Beth didn't even know if the job that she wanted existed. About a year before she

*I knew if I wanted to find an extraordinary job, I had to be an extraordinary candidate.*

graduated, she lamented that maybe statisticians were all cubicle-dwellers who had to work in offices without windows, forever. She wasn't sure if she even wanted the job that she was graduating into! But she stuck with it, got clear about what the ideal job would look like, and held on until she found it.

She wasn't just sitting around on her butt waiting for the job to walk into her living room, she was *out there trying to meet it.* But she had a very clear idea of what she was looking for, and was willing to search high and low to find it.

"I had a spreadsheet," she explained. "I was going for 70 or so jobs, and I talked to every recruiter I could. The recruiter would post the job, I'd get in contact with them, and then ask them if they had anything else."

The job she ultimately ended up getting—the unicorn—was posted on a company's website by a recruiter who she had already talked to. The recruiter, being busy, hadn't put together that Beth was perfect for the job. When Beth contacted her to ask about it, the recruiter agreed she'd be great for it! She went through a quick interview process and landed the perfect job.

Part of the reason she was able to hold out for the right job was because she had built in a runway of time. She knew it was going to take several months to find the right position, even though she had graduated from a prestigious program with a Doctorate.

"I knew if I wanted to find an extraordinary job, I had to be an extraordinary candidate."

## From cube-life to classic cars:
## Russ—California

It was 15+ years ago. I was in my early 30s. I was
living in Point Richmond, CA with my girlfriend
Ingrid. Life was pretty good. We rented a nice
place, enjoyed being foodies, etc. We traveled
to Europe a couple of times. She was doing temp
work and going to school to be a career counselor.
We met when I was a corporate recruiter placing
finance and accounting professionals with top SF
companies. I had been doing that for about 5 years.
But I wasn't very good at it. Or I should say, I
wasn't good at playing the game. It was kind of
a slimy and back stabby business. And despite the
good money to be made, I wasn't feeling good about
myself. Eventually I was asked to leave, as I
wasn't "contributing" to the success of the firm.

I had always been a paycheck to paycheck person
that didn't know the meaning of the word "savings."
Being unexpectedly unemployed, I was panicked and
took the first job I could find. It was with Kaiser
Permanente in Oakland in their newly created IT
department. They needed HR people to help hire and
manage the hundreds of new employees coming in. I
was thrilled to have found a job! But it wasn't too
long into it that I found myself feeling hugely

depressed. It was two vast floors of cubicles as far as the eye could see. I had never been in that kind of environment. I used to have my own office on the 40th floor in downtown SF for crying out loud! I realized that I could/would get stuck here doing a job that was monotonous and that I'd end up hating. My performance degraded after a year or so and my manager gave me the boot. I came home feeling like it was the end of the world. The thought of job hunting again and just taking another office job made me feel sick.

Ingrid put on her career counseling hat, sat down with me and asked, "If you could do your dream job, what would it be?" I shrugged and embarrassedly said, "Well, I'd love to buy and sell vintage European cars." My dad was an amateur race car driver when he was young, and we had had many different and cool cars when I was growing up. I had been immersed in car culture from the day I was born and I knew everything there was to know about them, but I just considered it a hobby.

She looked at me with a straight face and said, "Well, what's keeping you from doing that? Is there a business in town that does that?" I was absolutely stunned. Was she serious?

There was a company called Fantasy Junction in Emeryville that I had visited many times with my dad that was filled with old cars that were on consignment. But how could I consider working there? Why would they hire me? My resume was all office work. And on and on with every excuse in the book for why I couldn't do it. She stopped me and said, "How about you go visit them. Ask to speak with the owner. Tell him about your passion and knowledge of cars and see if he needs any help. Even if it's just sweeping the floors. Tell him you could work part-time and for free, kind of like an intern so he can see what you're like and you can see what it's really like to work in that industry. What have you got to lose?" I couldn't come up with a valid reason not to try!

I was terrified. I doubted to my core that they would have a need, let alone hire me.

But the next day I marched in and basically asked for a job. Somehow without peeing my pants. To my utter astonishment the owner was really nice and offered me a job right then and there. It had basically been just him doing the sales for the company and he thought it would be a good idea to have a second hand man. I was in! I truly couldn't believe it and that it had been that easy. I had my DREAM job!

It was one of the best jobs I had ever had but it was also a "job" and came with all the same personality clashes and communication issues that are present in all companies. I worked there for five years. As much as I loved being around old cars and helping people buy their dreams, it was very much a "sales" job which I'm not well suited to and so ultimately I ended up leaving.

But, having done it, I had the confidence to move on and was able to pick and choose what I did next and have had many varied and interesting jobs since then.

# Find your jam

Each of us has some skill that is, yanno, kinda our *jam.* It's something that brings us energy and joy, and is personally fulfilling.

I'll give you an example: Russ, my husband, is a logistics person. He looooooves considering the logistics of packing, moving, building, ordering, organizing, planning, etc. Right now, he is in the process of moving our workshop for our soap company, building shelves, outfitting it with vents, and generally organizing the heck out of the business. He comes home excited to talk about what he built and how he is setting it up. He's inventing ways of purifying our wastewater to be pH-neutral, so it can go into the septic system.

That sounds awful to me. SNORE.

Yet these logistical tasks give him a great deal of personal fulfilment. He feels competent, positive, and productive. There's a real need for that kind of passion and energy, and I'm darn glad he feels so enthusiastic about it.

On the other hand, I like writing. I write all the time, constantly, in every possible circumstance. I also like learning new software, because I'm dazzled by the possibilities that new programs open up for me. I like playing with toys like phones with fancy cameras. I'm very well suited to be a marketing writer, to take our photos for Instagram, and work with designers on packaging.

Russ doesn't like writing. He feels bad at it, like it's futile. He finds learning new software tiresome and tedious.

People tend to comment on things that are our *jam* with statements like "Whoa, an amazing artist! You should do a show!"

We tend to feel especially fulfilled when we do things that are *our jam*. They bring us joy, and, in some weird back-of-the-mind tickle, we know this is tied to our life purpose.

For *years*, people have told me I should write a book. I know I'm a good writer. I know I have a book in me (and here we are!). But for *years* I didn't write a book. In fact, I didn't prioritize writing much in my life.

Oh sure, I knew I *should* prioritize writing and I even made sketches for a few books, but I didn't ever quite get to the real nitty gritty of sitting down to write for any great length of time. I hadn't really gone for it.

On my third or fourth listen of *The Success Principles*, by Jack Canfield (highly recommended), he talks about prioritizing what you love, and what you're good at. I thought, "Ok, I have to get serious about prioritizing what I'm good at—not accounting, not tracking stats in our business, not reaching out to press, not anything else... just writing."

It's hard. I'm not gonna lie to you. Writing is hard. But I'm leaning into the discomfort and doing it anyway.

What is *your jam*? What are you uniquely good at? Motivating people? Public speaking? Finding order in chaos? Creating effective processes?

# And your jam might still be in the jar!

Even after a whole career of doing something else, or nothing much, or at least nothing much inspiring or fulfilling, you can find exciting, compelling work. If you haven't found what you're looking for, *stay open to it.* Don't settle. Always explore. Always learn. Always investigate what you find interesting. Just because you haven't found your jam yet, doesn't mean you're not going to find it!

My friend Teresa, who is in her early 40s, was an admin for years, doing data entry for the human resources department for a major university. She thought of herself as technically proficient, but not geeky. She liked coloring in the lines, and data entry was just fine. It was part-time, it paid ok, and she left the work at work when she went home every day.

She didn't love the work, but she didn't hate it either. As she worked there, she kept investigating other interesting opportunities, changing departments once, into a grant department. Since she was at a university, she had a whole catalog of courses and certificate classes that were available to her, so she kept taking management classes, and various technical courses.

At the new grant department, under an encouraging manager, she found that—surprise!—she loves database management. She had been working in data entry all these years, *and what she loved was tangentially right under her nose.*

She took some courses in database management, and found that not only did she like database management in general, she really loves working with Wordpress. She redesigned the system for handling grants so it was in Wordpress, and started doing light web development work. She took some courses in web dev, and found that—double surprise!!—she loved web development work, too!

Last week, she wrote her boss to see if she could work her newfound love of web development into her official job. Her boss wrote back saying that she thought that was a great idea, and voila! She found a new career because she stayed open and curious about what was interesting to her, and she took the initiative to learn more about it. And ultimately, she went outside of her comfort zone and asked her boss if she could change her position to be more aligned with her self-development.

My friend didn't wait around for inspiration to strike, she struck for inspiration.

In many success books (too many to name, but check the references section for a list of some recommended ones), it's noted that successful people never stop learning. They read books, they investigate new concepts, they follow rabbit holes that interest them. I personally am always on the lookout for new courses that might inspire a new perspective, and am writing this from a Natural Foods Expo in Baltimore. I thought I could pick up some business tips (for our handmade soap business) and maybe meet some interesting people. Yeah, it costs money, but I'm working to make it worth our while. Part of what inspires me to get out there and participate is knowing I made the investment to be here.

Personal trainers know this. Gyms know this. Life coaches know this. What we make investments in, we value. So put some money where your intentions are and follow some inspiring rabbits down some holes!

## Sometimes you have to follow The Universe's lead

Some loves aren't meant to last forever. As someone who has changed jobs several times over my lifetime, and who will probably change several more times, I think there's nothing wrong with seeking fulfilling work even if that concept of fulfilling work changes over time.

You don't have to feel tied into a kind of work just because that's what you've done forever, and you don't have to feel compelled to leave the whole field just because you're burned out on one job. Sometimes you just have to stop and look at what path The Universe is laying in front of you.

When I left a Product Management job in the Bay Area, I was pretty sure I never wanted to work in Digital Media Product Management again. I had been badly burnt in my previous position at a startup and was ready to jump ship for good. The idea of working for another hand-waving "visionary" megalomaniac really disgusted me. It seemed, at the time, like a function of the job itself, not just the people I worked with. I decided that it was time to change careers.

I wasn't sure what I wanted to do, but I knew I didn't want to do digital work anymore. I was even looking seriously at becoming a school bus driver in a rural town where my friend lived.

My experience for the past several years—the pace, the management, and the work of being a Digital Product Manager—*sucked.* I didn't want to do it anymore, even if it meant I was going to be painfully broke and living with a friend for a while (my friend was gracious enough to offer his guest room while I figured stuff out).

But I got to the end of my meager savings, and I didn't have anything else lined up. I interviewed at ABC Family, at the encouragement of my friend. Even though it seemed like it had a high risk of being another sucky digital job, I got along with the person who would be my boss *spectacularly* well.

On the surface, it was a fine job working for a huge corporation (Disney), making quite a lot of money. But I had *promised* myself I wouldn't just zombie-shuffle into another Product Management job. I didn't want to be trapped.

Still, I needed the money. I took the job, mostly because The Universe had closed a lot of doors around me, and this one was open.

And to my surprise, it turned out to be an incredible opportunity, working with some of the most interesting, intelligent, and professional individuals I have ever had the pleasure of meeting. I still count several of them among my friends to this day.

I think The Universe was watching out for me in that particular circumstance, and I was really lucky I decided to go for it and take that job. I fell in love with digital media again, I saw the importance of having a great manager and mentor, and I got to work in content, which, as a writer, has always been my first love.

And that job ended up opening up the Oprah job for me, which was also, for a long time, a really fulfilling and amazing job. Until it wasn't, and it was time to open the doors to something else.

Sometimes, we have to take the lead that The Universe is offering, even if it doesn't look like something we'd like right away. If there are no other doors opening, we have to follow the open door. Once we're clear about the kind of life we want to lead (you did the last few exercises, right?), The Universe drives us there. Even if we don't know the exact path to it, we're still on the road.

## It's ok to change jams

Like riding underground between subway stops, we sometimes go through dark, blind, or boring times in our career journey. That's to be expected, and it's fine. As long as you still see what you love about the job, and you know that love is coming back, you know the train will get to the next station. It's ok to not love every minute of a job and still love the job.

But sometimes we get between subway stops, and the train breaks, and we're just stuck sitting in the dark, bored, and not going anywhere. If we just sit there on the broken train with our head down, *we will never move on.*

It's a weird sensation, because you *were* going somewhere, and this was totally the right train, but, well, it isn't the right train anymore.

If you sense that you're on a broken train between subway stops, don't just sit there staring at your shoes wishing the train would magically start working again. Get off the damn train and get on another one.

## There's so much more

I had to stop writing this chapter, because it was becoming another book. I wanted to talk about how to job stalk, how to become the extraordinary candidate for the extraordinary job, and how to bring your skills with you to every industry, to find rewarding, interesting, and fulfilling work wherever you go.

As much as I'd love to include all that, I'm going to have to close this chapter in saying that there's a job out there that can make you delighted. **No one should put up with an unfulfilling job or an unfulfilling life.**

Earlier today, I happened to run into a recruiter for mission-driven natural food companies, and she confirmed that no matter what your passion is, the right job is out there, and sometimes it's even *looking for you.*

1. Write down things that you're good at—things that are probably your jam. We all have multiple jams, so go ahead and go crazy if you have a lot.

2. Make a commitment to do more of the thing you're good at. Even if it's just 10% more every day, just make the commitment to do that one thing more.

day28

# BELIEVE IN MAGIC

This book is for cynics, so I know this part may be a little woo-woo for you. Feel free to skip it if you have an allergy to woo-woo stuff. But if you're open minded, there are some really amazing and confusingly effective things for you to add to your arsenal of tools.

I say they're "confusingly effective" because my skeptic brain *still* struggles to believe in these things fully, but I'm gonna say the correlation is pretty heavy duty.

In her *truly fantastic* book, *You Are a Badass*, Jen Sincero talks about God and how skeptical she was about God at first, and now she's basically riding the mechanical bull, fist in the air, yelling "hit it, Wayne!" to the operator.

That's kind of how this stuff is for me. It's all a little weird, but there's no denying that **it works**, so I keep doing it.

# Esoteric magic items

My friend Forest Nui Cobalt makes candles, talismans, bath spells, and incense that is charged with the spiritual energy of the astrological signs. I started buying her stuff because I always want to support my friends' budding small businesses, and she had a money candle, which I was particularly working on at the time.

I got the candle, and money started flowing in like mad. Every time I lit the candle, —bam.—more money. To the extent that I ordered more of them. And then more of them. Because if you have a thing that works, work it.

Since then, I have bought a talisman (which I wear daily) to help with my temperance. I bought it when I quit drinking and eating crap, and considering that I still haven't started up again... seems to be working. I bought some bath spells (I'm writing this book while under the spell of Quicksilver, which is supposed to help mental agility and clarity), some other types of candles, and some incense.

The Dang Stuff Works.

Is it the Devil's magic? No. I don't think so. She's a good witch and a good person. It seems terribly unlikely that the Devil would want much to do with her.

There are many other sources of magic of all angles, including the more direct and practical "aromatherapy" items (scents that make you feel a certain way due to their natural properties and evocative memories) all the way to talismen that you wear all the time. If this interests you, check out your local esoteric or witchcraft store. The shopkeepers in these establishments are generally very helpful.

## (Debatably magic, depending on your beliefs) prayer and gratitude

I have tried to keep this book pan-belief, so again, if you have an allergic reaction to God, please skip ahead.

I personally believe in God, and that Jesus was God's son come to Earth to try to help us be better people. If that's not what you believe, no problemo. I am not here to convert you to believe anything that you don't already believe.

I also believe that everything good in our lives is worthy of a sincere and heartfelt "thank you" to the Universal Force—however we experience that. Whether that's standing outside and whispering it in the wind's ear, or kneeling by our bed at night, or while opening meditation. There is so much good in the world, and in our individual lives, that it's possible to find good points to appreciate in even the darkest times.

Sometimes I ask God to help with clarity on an issue, for

direction, or for peace, but really, I feel like we're all so lucky that we're even alive, and that alone is worth thanking God for.

And if God isn't your thing, take a little time to just marvel at the magnificence of the universe, all the way down to the magnificence of a tiny cluster of flowers between a crack in the pavement. It is all amazing.

*I am so grateful for everything around me, the air I breathe, the people I know, the experiences I have had, and the blood flowing through my veins. I am grateful for the miracles in my past, and the miracles yet to come. And so it is.*

*If you feel called to do or try magic or prayer, go for it. If not, hey, free day!*

**Here's a simple prayer:**
I am so grateful for everything around me, the air I breathe, the people I know, the experiences I have had, and the blood flowing through my veins. I am grateful for the miracles in my past, and the miracles yet to come. And so it is.

# Getting on the horse so you can decide if you like riding horses

For the past several years, I have been kind of obsessed with Wild West culture. It represents a rugged freedom, an appreciation of nature, and a Devil-may-care rambunctiousness that seems to be missing from the heavy realities of modern life.

A big part of Western and Wild West culture is riding horses, and I've long fantasized about getting a horse and ridin' the trail at sunset, unpackin' my saddle, and settlin' on the side o' the dirt path for a good l'il lie down.

When I was a kid, I rode horses. I even achieved some low-level ribbons in my competitions. But a couple moderately traumatic things happened (including having a horse try to buck me off, and losing control of a galloping horse, among other things), and I got off the horse.

With my newfound Western interest, though, I thought I should give horse riding another try. Certainly there must be something to all these photos of powerful and positive cowgirls, grinning from under their hats, as their trusty and beloved horses marched dutifully forward.

I looked up local horse instruction and found a place that specialized in horse therapy. This seemed likely to have some horses that would provide positive riding experiences, not re-creations of the reasons I stopped riding in the first place.

First, it turns out that women of my size are "large" for riding horses, so they gave me a large black horse named Pepper. Pepper was *immense* and "spirited," which they said was ok since I am an "experienced rider" (nevermind that the experience in question was 30 years ago). I immediately felt a bond with Pepper: neither she nor I wanted to do this. We had a common interest, which was getting the heck away from that saddle and never discussing the issue again.

But I wanted to see this through, so I put Pepper through the humiliating task of getting saddled and girdled and bridled. She rolled her eyes at me, and I patted her neck, trying to reassure her that this was just part of the trials that humans and horses must endure together.

Second, Pepper had her own ideas of how she wanted the ride to go, which was fast. "Oh, she never gallops like that!" the cheerful instructor called to me while we were sprinting down the straight side of the corral, heading to apparently jump the fence. "She must really like you!" Ah, this is what "being liked" by a horse felt like. (I wasn't so sure.)

I remembered my former horse training pretty quickly, and yanked on the reins, saying "WHOA." Pepper halted with such precision that I almost fell forward. And with my former horse training fully flooding back to me, I was able to take control of this new "friend," and lead her around the ring with great authority and conviction, looking where we wanted to go, and guiding her with her lead and some gentle foot nudges (and kicks). Now that I was dominant, I had her respect and attention... and it felt *awful*. I felt like *such an asshole.*

At the end of the lesson, I led Pepper back to the barn. I took off her saddle and brushed her, toweling off where she was sweaty (since it was a warm day). I noticed there were some places worn bare in her fur and wondered if those were hotspots when I was riding. We led her to the field and I took off her lead, and I let her go into the field.

She immediately ran out into the grass, prancing like a kid running into Disneyland, and fell over onto her back and started rolling like a happy dog on a decaying fish carcass. She was free! Hoorah!

It was wonderful to watch her so happy, having absolutely *nothing* to do with me.

Later, when I was leaving the center, I took a picture of her grazing in the field, the sky as blue as it could get. She was far from the edges of the fence, standing with a smaller horse (as all horses really probably are, next to Pepper), and I felt happy for her.

## Horseback riding wasn't for me

I was pretty sure I'd enjoy horseback riding, but I didn't. I'm so glad I gave it a try, though, since now I know.

I have also tried:
- Skydiving (not for me)
- Tending goats (pretty fun, actually!)
- Making soap (which subsequently led me to a full-on business, which is running today)
- Shrimp heads (not for me)
- Knitting (not my thing)
- Every diet known to humankind (varying interest)
- Shaving my head (glad hair grows back)
- Countless other things

Basically, if it seems even remotely interesting, I'll give it a try. If I don't like it, no big deal. If I do like it, great! I can incorporate that into my life.

## Finding things that are for you

It takes *so little time and energy* to try something out, and then you'll know if you like it or not. So go on and give a thing a try to see if you like it!

ACTION STEPS:

*1. Make a list of things you've always wanted to try but, for whatever reason, haven't done them.*

*2. Next to each item, write the smallest first step you can take to try that thing out.*

*3. Do one of the first steps. Voila! You're on your way!*

## My Action Steps...

| | |
|---|---|
| I want to ride a camel in the desert | I could find out if there are camels in India that I could ride when I go there in January |
| I want to go white water rafting | I could look up white water rafting near me |
| I want to grow my hair down to my butt | I could just not cut my hair, and take extra amazing care of it, and take supplements for its health |
| I want to spend a month on a beach with Russ and the dogs, working (writing?) from there | I could find a beach property that might want to do a month-long swap with us in our mountain home? Maybe? |
| I want to write and publish a book | HA! Doing it! |

**LIFE IS MEANT TO BE LIVED**

W e're at the end of your 30 days, but we're at the beginning of your life.

You can, of course, go back and review the things you have done during this book, but I want to part with this thought: Life is meant to be lived. It's meant to help you learn who you are supposed to become, and be *most* yourself, and the only way to do it is to take risks and go for it.

Life isn't always going to be comfortable. In the course of finding your adventure, you're going to experience all the richness and excitement and disappointingness and grittiness that life can offer. You might move to places that turn out to be not awesome places to live. You might leave a reasonably stable job for something that you think you'll love, but that turns out to not at all be for you. You might spend some sleepless nights wondering why you made the decisions you did, reacted the way you did, or "ruined everything." (Side note: as long as you're alive, you have never ruined everything.)

All of this is part of life.

We fall in love and have our hearts broken over and over. It's what makes us human, and it's worth it.

I will always encourage you to take the new and different path. I will always encourage you to take risks and see how things go, rather than make assumptions and cut off opportunity.

You are unique. No one in the world has the perspective that you do, or the heart to pursue what you want to pursue. It's up to you. If you do not bring your contribution into this world by being the most thorough version of yourself possible, not only is the world missing out on the full experience of you, *you* are missing out on the amazing person you will become, the experiences you'll have, the inspiration you'll share, and everything that life has to offer.

It is all here for you, but it is fading like a flower.

# Go out and be a you-nicorn.

# RESOURCES

There are many great books in the world, and these are the ones I have found most helpful in my journey. I recommend them to you.

**In order of recommendedness...**

*You are a Badass: How to Stop Doubting Your Greatness and Start Living an Awesome Life* by Jen Sincero

Summary: A straightforward manual for building self-esteem and setting your life on the powerful path.

*Orbiting the Giant Hairball: A Corporate Fool's Guide to Surviving with Grace* by Gordon MacKenzie

Summary: How to be creative and support other creative individuals in the workplace.

*Braving the Wilderness: The Quest for True Belonging and the Courage to Stand Alone* by Brené Brown

Summary: How to be true to yourself even when you're very, very, very, very alone, and having to be courageous.

*How to Win Friends and Influence People* by Dale Carnegie

Summary: A very dated classic, yet there are no modern books its equal. Outlines how to be a good person, at the most basic level.

*Do The Work* by Steven Pressfield

Summary: A must-read for anyone who struggles with writing or any other project that requires sustained attention over time.

*On Writing: A Memoir of the Craft* by Stephen King

Summary: An autobiographical account of King's relationship with writing. Inspiring, heartfelt, and honest.

*If at Birth You Don't Succeed: My Adventures with Disaster and Destiny* by Zach Anner

Summary: A brilliantly written autobiography from a comedian featured on the Oprah Winfrey Network, and his own YouTube channel, among other things. Tremendously inspiring, and laugh-out-loud funny.

*The Success Principles(TM): How to Get from Where You Are to Where You Want to Be* by Jack Canfield and Janet Switzer

Summary: Essential factors for a successful life, however you define that.

*The Autobiography of Benjamin Franklin* by Benjamin Franklin

Summary: It turns out that this old white guy was a pretty amazing dude with some pretty ground-breaking ideas. I tried doing a modern translation of his book a couple years ago and may get around to it yet, but for now, read the original.

*Loving What Is: Four Questions that can Change Your Life* by Byron Katie and Stephen Mitchell

Summary: Learn to react logically to any situation, no matter how emotional.

*The Four Spiritual Laws of Prosperity: A Simple Guide to Unlimited Abundance* by Edwene Gaines

Summary: How to be prosperous through spiritual means and actually make the world a better place. - or - You don't have to be a soulless a-hole to be rich.

*Bird by Bird: Some Instructions on Writing and Life* by Anne Lamott

Summary: Essential instruction for writers.

*Rising Strong: How the Ability to Reset Transforms the Way We Live, Love, Parent, and Lead* by Brené Brown

Summary: Both research-based and heart-based, this book will transform how you see your own ability to recover from failures and trauma.

*The Art of Exceptional Living (audio only)* by Jim Rohn

Summary: A collection of inspiring talks on how to seize control of your life and do better.

Made in the USA
San Bernardino, CA
05 October 2018